FOLLOWING IN THE FOOTSTEPS
OF
HENRY TUDOR

FOLLOWING IN THE FOOTSTEPS OF

HENRY TUDOR

A HISTORICAL JOURNEY FROM PEMBROKE TO BOSWORTH

PHIL CARRADICE

PEN & SWORD
HISTORY

AN IMPRINT OF PEN & SWORD BOOKS LTD.
YORKSHIRE – PHILADELPHIA

First published in Great Britain in 2019 by
Pen and Sword History
An imprint of
Pen & Sword Books Ltd
Yorkshire - Philadelphia

Copyright © Phil Carradice, 2019

ISBN 978 1 52674 330 5

The right of Phil Carradice to be identified as Author of this work has been
asserted by him in accordance with the Copyright, Designs and Patents Act 1988.

A CIP catalogue record for this book is available from the British Library.

Typeset in Ehrhardt MT Std 11.5/14 by
Aura Technology and Software Services, India

Printed and bound in the UK by TJ International Ltd.

Pen & Sword Books Ltd incorporates the Imprints of Pen & Sword Books
Archaeology, Atlas, Aviation, Battleground, Discovery, Family History, History,
Maritime, Military, Naval, Politics, Railways, Select, Transport, True Crime,
Fiction, Frontline Books, Leo Cooper, Praetorian Press, Seaforth Publishing,
Wharncliffe and White Owl.

For a complete list of Pen & Sword titles please contact

PEN & SWORD BOOKS LIMITED
47 Church Street, Barnsley, South Yorkshire, S70 2AS, England
E-mail: enquiries@pen-and-sword.co.uk
Website: www.pen-and-sword.co.uk

or

PEN AND SWORD BOOKS
1950 Lawrence Rd, Havertown, PA 19083, USA
E-mail: Uspen-and-sword@casematepublishers.com
Website: www.penandswordbooks.com

For Dad, who would not have believed a word of it, but would have enjoyed it anyway.

Contents

A Note on Language

Books, reports and writings from the period covered in this book are relatively rare. The Battle of Bosworth Field, for example, while often written about in hindsight, is probably the most poorly recorded or reported battle from the entire length of the fifteenth and sixteenth centuries – at least as far as contemporary accounts are concerned.

To find books, articles and papers from the early days of Henry Tudor is no easy task. They do exist, however, and often give a fascinating view of the times, even if that view or perspective is sometimes rather biased. Writers like Polydore Vergil, for example, have helped create the negative view that most of us, Shakespeare included, have on Richard III while at the same time puffing up the character of Henry – who, it must be remembered, was his patron.

Where quotations from contemporary sources are included in the text of this book – in particular from the writings of Vergil, lines from 'The Ballad of Bosworth Field' and the anonymous Life of Sir Rhys ap Thomas – I have not attempted to change either the language or the spellings. As a consequence they are presented here as they would have been read when the Tudor dynasty was either still in place or was fondly remembered.

Vergil, in particular, was writing in the early sixteenth century, a time that was only a hundred years since Chaucer had produced The Canterbury Tales. However, already the English language as we know it today was beginning to take shape and Vergil's words seem to be light years away from those of Chaucer. Another hundred years and we have the remarkable prose and poetry of Shakespeare which are really modern English in style and spelling. Vergil fits between the two.

Even so, as far as Vergil is concerned there are notable differences from the spellings and intonations that we use today. That is part of their charm.

The words, phrases and sentences are not difficult to read and seem to me to be more in keeping with the times. So, there are no apologies from me, at least at this stage. Read the quotes and see for yourselves.

Introduction

The early life of King Henry VII of England, Harri or Henry Tudor as he is often known, is shrouded in mystery and confusion. His birth, his childhood and adolescence, his escape and flight from Wales, his time as an exile in Brittany and France, his return to his native land and the march to a stunning victory at the Battle of Bosworth Field – the litany is long and none of it is quite as straightforward or as clear as you might expect.

There are very few records from the time of Henry's birth and adolescence. Not only that, there are almost no first-hand accounts of events leading up to the Battle of Bosworth Field on 22 August 1485. The defeat of King Richard and the establishment of the Tudor dynasty have become shrouded in legend, so much so that it is hard to know where the truth stops and the stories begin.

One of the few nearly contemporaneous accounts of the events leading up to Bosworth comes in Polydor Vergil's *Anglica Historia*. An Italian humanist who lived most of his life in England, Vergil's book was commissioned by Henry after he became king. Although Vergil attempts to provide an accurate, unbiased account of the Wars of the Roses it must be remembered that he was writing for the Tudors. His view of Richard III, whom he calls 'ambitious, devious and wicked', is in complete contrast to his portrait of Henry. It is no more than you would expect.

Vergil's account of the times, however, remains perhaps the best and most accurate retelling of the events that sent Henry into exile and then brought him back again. It is admittedly a second-hand account, but he spent twenty-six years on the project, spoke with many of those involved (including Henry) and tried to be as objective as possible. Within the confines of the remit he was given, his book is about as good as it gets.

Introduction

The poems or ballads from the time were written by men who were, in general, not connected with the court and while accurate in some respects, were generally the view of ordinary, often uneducated, members of society who were usually more intent on selling a few broadsheets at the fair than in providing an accurate historical account. The anonymous 'Ballad of Bosworth Field' is an exception and contains much useful information.

Holinshed's 'Chronicles' and the 'Crowland Chronicles' are also useful primary sources. Holinshed wrote his book in the middle years of the sixteenth century, which does not make it any less accurate or honest. Shakespeare, as we know, used his work to fuel his own literary and artistic endeavours. The 'Crowland Chronicles' were produced much nearer the date of the battle, probably 1486.

Apart from Vergil and the bards there are legends, tales, stories, call them what you will, and they are there by the score. The story of Henry's journey to Bosworth is littered with tales of bridges under which his supporters supposedly lay in order for Henry to march across their bodies and so preserve their honour and false promises of loyalty to King Richard III; gifts and pensions the Tudor earl dished out and houses where he paused on his march to Bosworth are commonplace; secret dealings between Henry and Richard's noblemen are there by the score. The legends continue to proliferate.

It is understandable. The Tudor dynasty lasted for 122 years, providing highs and lows that remain unmatched in British history. Characters like Henry VIII, Edward VI, Bloody Mary and Elizabeth could have come straight out of the pages of an historical novel. The founder of the dynasty, Henry Tudor, is no less fascinating but with a virtual absence of contemporary accounts it is a matter of separating truth from fiction. Pontification abhors a vacuum and in the absence of hard historical fact, legends and fantasy stories will grow.

Most of the stories about Richard and Henry have little or no provenance but they have remained in the public arena for many years. Some have been accepted at face value and some have twisted our perception of the first Tudor king and his rise to power. Even the precise site of the battle that ended the Wars of the Roses is now open for debate and discussion.

Perhaps that is what makes Henry Tudor such a fascinating character. For years he has been overshadowed by his children and grandchildren who, on the surface at least, are more colourful. That is both over-simplistic and unfair to Henry Tudor.

The traditional view of the first Tudor monarch is of a grasping, cold-hearted miser who achieved the throne by luck as much as by judgement, and used his innate cunning to hold on to it. Unpopular with his subjects he nevertheless managed to stabilise the country after years of bloodshed, mayhem and warfare. There are elements of truth in that judgement but as with any sweeping statement, it is only elements.

Henry VII might have been 'tight' with money – perhaps just as well considering how quickly his son Henry VIII spent it – but he was also an astute and capable diplomat. He was magnanimous in victory, was brave and courageous and clearly driven by what he felt was best for the country as a whole. As the founder of the dynasty he, Harri Tudor, Earl of Richmond, not those who served or came after him, was undoubtedly a man for all seasons.

Henry Tudor was a cautious individual but, when the occasion demanded it, he was not averse to taking a gamble. Much of his life, from his fourteen years in exile to the march on Bosworth, had been a gamble. It was just a matter of considering the odds and then playing the game according to the cards that were turned up.

Fact or fiction, truth or legend, the story of Henry Tudor's journey to Bosworth Field – all twenty-eight years of it, from his birth to that fateful moment when he was presented with the crown on the battlefield – made him the person he was. It was as much a pilgrimage as a march to battle, something that Henry knew and played on.

It is interesting to note that Henry rarely used the name Tudor. He called himself the Earl of Richmond. Richard was the one who constantly called him Tudor, as an insult or as a way of reminding him, and the public, of the lowly Welsh origins of his family.

As the opening salvo of a reign and the creation of the most powerful dynasty in English history, you cannot do better than Henry's landing and subsequent campaign. His footsteps are well worth recounting, worth following. That way lies the man's power; that way lies the true glory of the Tudors.

A Personal Prologue

I was born and raised in the tiny community of Pennar just outside Pembroke Dock, a bare two miles from the town and castle of Pembroke. From the bottom of my garden I could see the mighty walls of the castle and in the summer holidays my friends and I loved nothing better than scrambling over its giant keep and towers.

We all knew the significance of the castle, stories of Earl William Marshall, Richard Strongbow and the 1648 siege by Oliver Cromwell having been drummed into us by teachers over the course of our primary school years. Above all we knew it as the birthplace of King Henry VII.

That, almost by default, made us honorary Lancastrians. We knew which side to support in the Roses cricket match and we knew for certain who had killed the Princes in the Tower – and it wasn't Henry Tudor. It was all a done deal as far as we were concerned. Apart, that is, from one thing – my father.

Having been brought up in Barnard Castle he was a Yorkist through and through. His views were far from commonplace in those days – Richard III was betrayed at Bosworth Field, let down by his nobles, men he considered his friends, men who switched sides at an opportune moment. I couldn't deny that – although I wasn't too sure about the 'friends' thing – having read over and over about the perfidy of the Stanleys and the Earl of Northumberland.

But when Dad got onto the Princes in the Tower, there I had to leave him. Why would Henry kill them, I would ask? His reply was simple. He couldn't let them live, they would have been potential rivals for his throne. When I protested that Richard would have been faced by the same problem, he would have none of it. Richard was a courtly, knightly, even saintly man, he would declare, who had done his best for the good of the country.

I hadn't then seen the stage play, but what about Richard as the evil crookback of the film, the Lawrence Olivier thing? I would ask. Shakespearean and Tudor propaganda, he would insist. Richard never had a humped back; that was painted onto his portrait at a later date. And so it went on, right up until the day he died.

I think he would have enjoyed the razzmatazz around the discovery of Richard's body in the Leicester car park. He would have nodded happily when the 2013 DNA tests confirmed the identity of the remains although, in light of the deformed spine of the skeleton, he may have been forced to rethink his opinion on Richard's physical appearance.

The point is, I have always been fascinated by Henry VII and must confess to at least a degree of partiality to the Tudor side of the argument. But the debates and discussions between my father and me, heated, logical or just downright biased, show how the clash of the two contenders for the throne, 500 years ago, still has the power to enthral and push people to the limits of credibility.

I promised my father that one day I would write about the Yorkist and Lancastrian claimants to the throne of England. This is it. I have tried, unlike Henry's chronicler Polydore Vergil, to be as objective as I can but if a little bias slips into the telling of the tale I can only apologise. The one thing those discussions with Dad managed to achieve was to polarise my opinions – just like his.

Chapter One

A Homecoming

The young man stood at the quarterdeck rail, watching with fascination as the waves rolled in towards the ship. There were no breakers, just peaks and troughs of blue-green sea that seemed to roll on forever. Even as he watched the waves sweep past, he saw deep caverns opening up in front of his eyes. They were vast, those caverns; shafts of light and dark that seemed to be carved deeply into the water, diving down to the sea bed. He was being fanciful, he told himself, but he was unable to stop his thoughts, unable to drag his eyes away from the mesmerising ocean.

Elegantly, easily, the long swells of water swept along the sides of the ship's wooden hull and then disappeared rapidly astern. There was no relief. As soon as one had cruised effortlessly past it was replaced by another, and then another.

'Like charging horsemen,' the young man murmured to himself, shaking his head. 'No holding back, no respite, running on for ever.'

His long brown hair hung low across his forehead, dancing around his shoulders in the wind. One or two strands stuck to his cheek where the spray had already dampened his face. He reached up and carefully detached them. He did everything carefully, each movement or action calculated for its effect long before it had begun.

He was above average height and slender, but there was an obvious latent power and strength in his arms. Even so, it was his eyes, cold-blue and sober, that caught the attention of anyone who came face to face with him. Love him or hate him, you would not willingly want to cross this man. Now those distinctive and powerful eyes switched from the sea to the coastline ahead of him.

The land that he saw was solid and tangible, almost touchable where long low cliffs and golden beaches sparkled in the afternoon sunlight. The beaches

1

of home, he grinned to himself. If Jasper or any of his bondsmen could have guessed what he was thinking they would have been shocked. The young man was not given to poetic images or flights of fancy. He was practical, he was a doer. Give him a problem and he would sort it out. But metaphors and images, no. Best leave them to the bards of Duke Francis and his court.

'Three hours,' he whispered, 'no more.'

He stretched his arms above his head, straining every muscle in his body, and grunted with the effort. It would be good to get ashore. Six days on board ship was enough for anyone. Water was for fish; men were intended for more solid things like earth and rock. His flagship, the *Poulian de Dieppe*, had been a good vessel and her captain Guillaume de Casenove a more than capable officer. But still, it would be good to get off this lurching, creaking thing of wood and ropes, to feel firm ground beneath his feet again.

He glanced back at the other ships in the convoy, nearly thirty of them. He could not bring himself to call it an armada, but that was what it was: his armada. He could tell, without looking too closely, that not everyone had enjoyed the same comfort as him during the voyage. The way that the smaller vessels dug their prows into the swells – gentle as they were – told him that they were shipping water, copious amounts of it.

It was not necessarily a bad thing; the men would be eager for dry land and for the somewhat less watery march to come. He shuddered as he thought of that march – a week, two perhaps? And at the end there would be a battle against King Richard and his troops. He did not know where. Richard would choose the time and place, but a battle there would certainly be.

He wondered, briefly, how his own men would cope, wondered how many Welshmen would, as he expected, come flocking to his standard. Then he thrust the concern away. It was not a problem he could solve; at least not yet.

He swung around and glared again at the coast. Just over there, off the starboard beam, lay Tenby, the port where he had left Britain fourteen years before. Soon, he knew the broad beach and sand hills of Freshwater would materialise and then the Haven would open up before them. His spies had already told him that the area was poorly defended, but he would take no chances. Richard of Gloucester – King Richard as he had styled himself – was a master of deception and intrigue. He would wait and see what lay in store.

He felt, rather than saw, a presence behind him and spun around to face the man he knew would never be far away. Jasper Tudor had been there, at his shoulder, almost all of his life, watching over him and protecting; Jasper Tudor, his uncle, his defender and friend. Jasper Tudor, not to put too fine a point on it, his surrogate father figure. The bluff old man put out his giant of a hand and placed it on his nephew's shoulder.

'Not long now, Harri,' he growled. 'It will be good to be home.'

Harri shrugged off his uncle's hand. 'Home – really? Duke Francis's castle at Suscinio has been my home for the last fourteen years – certainly more of a home to me than Pembroke.'

'Perhaps,' Jasper said, 'but we need these people, don't we?'

He broke off and gestured at the coast of West Wales. The cliffs were rugged and dangerous, a clear barrier to anyone who did not know the area.

'These Welsh, we need them to think of us as their saviours. You are Y Mab Darogan, the Son of Prophesy, come to relieve their suffering after years of English brutality and over-lordship. We need their support if we are ever going to defeat Richard. Never forget that, Harri.'

Harri nodded. 'I won't, uncle. Believe me, what I say to you and what I say for the people are two very different things.'

'Good. Now, let's put some food in our bellies before we take that first step ashore.'

He turned and went down the companionway. Harri Tudor followed him, pausing briefly to gaze once more at the land off their starboard bow. Despite what he had told Jasper, it was good to be home. This time, he knew, he was home for good.

X X X

As he had waited on the deck of the *Poulian de Dieppe*, gazing out at the Pembrokeshire coast, Henry Tudor could have been excused for thinking that the world – his world, anyway – was one of confusion and chaos. From the moment of his birth, twenty-eight years before, he had experienced only warfare, bloodshed and disaster.

He had never known his father, and the seemingly endless series of battles and skirmishes that made up the Wars of the Roses had consumed the minds and deeds of almost everyone he had ever encountered. It had been a dark and bloody time.

3

This return from exile in Brittany and France was a gamble, he knew that. But if it succeeded it would bring order, not just to the fractured and disordered life he had led for so long, but to the whole of Britain. Much depended on the next few weeks.

Harri and Jasper sat in the stern cabin of the ship and ate. They did not speak; there was much to ponder, much to worry about. Thirty ships and two or three thousand soldiers, most of them French mercenaries – was that enough to take on the might of Richard's army?

Above all Henry – Harri as most of those close to the last Lancastrian prince always called him – was conscious of his short comings as a military leader. He was no soldier. That he certainly knew; he was reminded of it every time he pulled on his armour or picked up his sword. Competent, yes, he could hold his own in a skirmish or joust; but highly skilled, certainly not.

Commanding an army, that was something else again. He had not been seriously trained in the arts of generalship, was not experienced or blooded in battle like Richard of Gloucester, the most celebrated soldier in the whole of England. And despite his belief in the justness of his cause, Harri was plagued by the simple worry or concern – when the meeting with Richard came, as it undoubtedly would, was his level of ability really good enough?

As if sensing his nephew's thoughts, Jasper threw down his crust of bread, drained his goblet and reached over for the leather wine bottle.

'It will be fine,' he grunted, 'I promise you. We have right on our side.'

Harri shrugged. He smiled at the older man and took the proffered cup. He raised it in salute, and then drank deeply.

'Perhaps – but Richard of Gloucester probably thinks the same thing. I suppose all soldiers going into battle have to believe that they have God on their side.'

Jasper shook his head. He was used to Harri's moments of indecision, his doubts and fears. The young man was right to have them. After all, defeat in the coming campaign would undoubtedly spell the end for him and for the House of Lancaster. Richard of Gloucester was not renowned for his charity or mercy, so Harri was right to have concerns. As long as he did not display those doubts on the field of battle, Jasper thought, all would be well.

They sat on as the sun sank lower and lower in the western sky and Harri felt his eyes closing with drowsiness. From outside in the companionway came a sudden slapping of feet on the wooden decking and the cabin door swung open. Guillaume de Casenove stood in the opening. He was a tall man and had to stoop in the low entrance to his cabin.

'We are off St Ann's Head,' he declared. 'Milford Haven lies before us.'

The two Tudors hauled themselves to their feet and followed the captain up to the main deck. It was as the Frenchman had said. Off the port beam the giant cliffs of St Ann's Head towered above them and the Milford waterway stretched ahead, calm and flat in the evening sunlight.

'We have had favourable winds all the way,' Jasper growled. 'It is right we should have fine weather to disembark. It's an omen.'

'Aye,' said de Casenove, nodding his head. 'We've had a good voyage, right enough. I've never seen the sea around here so calm. And none of Richard's damned ships lying in wait for us. Like you say, my Lord, it is a good omen.'

Omen or not, Harri said to himself, they had arrived. He thought back to his distant education, to the stories he had loved and had first encountered when he was just 3 or 4 years old. He vividly remembered sitting, spellbound, in the courtyard of nearby Pembroke Castle as his nurse, with her lilting Welsh accent, wove a tapestry of stories that would have captivated any red-blooded son of Lancaster.

He remembered sitting there in the warmth of a Welsh summer and being read tales about Julius Caesar, Pompey the Great and the Gallic Wars. Now, like Caesar he had crossed the Rubicon and fate – his fate, the fate of his soldiers, the fate of the whole country come to that – lay in his hands. He welcomed the challenge.

'We should heave-to and wait for the morning, sir,' said Guillaume de Casenove. 'It will be safer that way. There are no ships in the Haven; we have all the time in the world.'

Harri shook his head and reached out to squeeze the Captain's shoulder.

'It has begun,' he said, grinning at Jasper and de Casenove, 'the final stage. I'm damned if I am going to wait for the morning. Let us find the best place to put our troops ashore. We will do it tonight. Then we can march on London and Richard.'

Chapter Two

The Wars of the Roses

Henry Tudor was born in Pembroke Castle on 28 January 1457. It was a difficult birth, Henry's mother Margaret Beaufort being just 14 years old and small in stature. For a while it seemed as if neither mother nor baby would survive the traumatic experience, but both of them were fighters and both were determined to cling to life.

How a 14-year-old girl came to mighty Pembroke Castle in the farthest corner of West Wales in order to give birth to the boy who would grow to become the founder of the Tudor dynasty is a tale worth telling. It is also essential knowledge if we are to understand the man and the period – and follow properly in his footsteps.

The arrival in the world of Henry Tudor marked the beginning of the greatest royal dynasty the country had ever seen. But before that dynasty could even begin to take shape there was the little matter of a civil war to deal with. This civil war, a seemingly endless series of battles and power-grabs between the members and supporters of the two royal houses, Lancaster and York, had consumed the country for many years. Thousands of men, nobles and commoners alike, had died in the conflict that had destroyed the stability of the country.

Enshrined in British history as the Wars of the Roses after the emblems of the two houses – the white rose of Lancaster, the red rose of York – the campaigns and battles, the political machinations and intrigue of this fifty-year period were violent and intense. The troubles went on and on, so much so that it sometimes seemed as though they would never end.

The causes of the Wars of the Roses were many and varied. Even now when the Wars are viewed with the benefits of hindsight, the reasons why they should have erupted remain rooted in a somewhat confusing period in British history. On the most basic level they could be said to have arisen directly from the unexpected and sudden death of a great and famous king.

Henry V was a member of the royal House of Lancaster, a superb war leader and a charismatic figure in medieval England. His death was a premature demise that robbed the country of perhaps the most dynamic ruler it had seen in many years and left it in the hands of a minor who was physically and emotionally unfit for the task.

Henry died at the Chateau de Vincennes on 22 August 1422. He had cut a marvellous, almost mystical swathe across Europe, defeating the French at Agincourt and subsequently marrying Catherine de Valois, daughter of the French king. Charles VI of France might have been half mad but he had sense enough to realise that Henry, a warlord of unparalleled skill, represented the best chance of peace for his troubled people.

The Treaty of Troyes confirmed that, following his marriage, Henry was to become heir to Charles and that, in addition to his own kingdom, on the death of the French king he would become ruler of France and all of her many territories. The Treaty seemed as if it might finally bring the Hundred Years War to an end with an English victory.

There was only one flaw in the scheme – dysentery! It was a disease that Henry had contracted during the siege of Meaux and it managed to achieve what warriors across half of Europe had failed to do, kill off the English king.

Henry had ruled for just nine years and was succeeded by his son, the 9-month-old Henry VI. Just two months later Charles VI of France also died. It meant that the infant boy was now monarch of two of the most powerful nations in Europe. That, at least, was the theory. After the madness of Charles, and following long years of misrule, France was a fractured and disordered kingdom that clearly needed a strong hand if it was to be brought into line.

As far as England was concerned trouble and discontent were bubbling just below the surface. A strong king like Henry V had kept things in check – mainly by taking his troublesome barons off to war – but now his dynamic leadership had gone. Henry VI might be king but in reality power and control rested in the hands of a council led by Henry V's two brothers John, Duke of Gloucester, and Humphrey, Duke of Bedford.

Queen Catherine, ever conscious of her status and, in particular, the position of her infant son, found herself marginalised by the

English noblemen. She was, after all, a foreigner – not only that, she was a young and beautiful foreigner who might well choose to marry again. If that should ever happen, the potential for rival claims to the throne of England was something that the leaders of the council did not dare to think too closely about.

When concerns emerged about a possible alliance and union between Catherine and Edmund Beaufort, the Duke of Somerset, in 1428, there was a minor panic in the realm. Somerset was the sworn enemy of the Duke of Gloucester and so, at his behest, a statute was hurried through Parliament forbidding any nobleman to marry a widowed queen without the express permission of the king. As Henry VI was still a minor and therefore unable to grant such permission it effectively prohibited Catherine from marrying for many years.

At that point a squire from an obscure Welsh family entered the picture. In the words of Thomas Penn, Owen Tudor was nothing more than 'a charming, fast talking Welsh chamber servant of Catherine.' (Thomas Penn: *Winter King*, p.3) He was what modern idiom would call 'a chancer', and when the opportunity came he seized it with eager hands.

Fast talking he may have been, but Owen Tudor had no possessions or personal fortune. His family had no influence or standing at court and his future was, at best, uncertain. He could easily have drifted along in obscurity with little in the way of good fortune or possessions to help him forge a place in the world.

What Owen Tudor did have, however, was charm; bucket loads of it. He was dashing and handsome and he and the queen were thrown together, as much by chance as by design. Inevitably they fell in love. They were secretly married, something that was now beyond both the law and propriety. However, Owen was no nobleman, he was a commoner, and so managed to avoid the punishment and fines laid down in the statute of 1428.

As a Welshman, Owen Tudor was also a man of low status and position but, as Chris Skidmore has commented, that was something he was determined to change:-

> In 1432 he petitioned Parliament to be granted an exemption
> from the traditional restrictions placed upon Welshmen that
> treated him effectively as a second-class citizen.
>
> (Skidmore: Bosworth, the Birth of the Tudors.)

Once approval was granted Owen was finally considered a true English citizen, but such acclaim was to be short lived. While Catherine soon gave birth to two sons, half-brothers to the king, her life was short and on 3 January 1437 she died at Bermondsey Abbey. Owen, without the protection of his wife, soon found himself in custody as the Duke of Gloucester took his revenge on a man he considered inferior in every way.

Owen Tudor spent the next few years in various prisons, escaping and being recaptured, before being granted a pardon by the king. But it was on the shoulders of his two sons, Edmund and Jasper, that the fortunes of the Tudor family were to rest during what was to become one of the most dramatic and brutal civil conflicts ever to afflict Britain – the Wars of the Roses.

X X X

As he grew into adulthood it became obvious that King Henry VI was weak and simple-minded, a man who preferred studying religious books and manuscripts to governing the country. There was nothing intrinsically wrong with that, but in his position philosophy and the scriptures should have been lower on the list of priorities. His judgement was poor and, without his mother as a guide, he was invariably victim to the strongest and most recent opinions presented to him.

Henry's wife, the young, dynamic Margaret of Anjou was, like Henry, keen to bring a lasting peace to her husband's joint kingdoms and was more than happy to use her influence, both with Henry and with her French relatives, to achieve this end. Letters from the monarch – probably originating from Margaret – to the French king secretly promised to give back English conquests in Maine and Anjou. When those promises became known they were concessions that infuriated the English nobility.

When the Duke of Gloucester, the final surviving brother of Henry V, died in February 1447 there seemed to be nobody left to put any sort of check on the highly laudable but totally impractical plans of the king. Slowly but surely the country slipped towards civil war.

Much to his annoyance, Richard, Duke of York, the commander of the English armies in France, was suddenly recalled and sent to Ireland while the king – now out of his minority – negotiated with his French counterpart. The new French monarch, Charles VII, was certainly more astute than Henry and used the subsequent truce to build up his forces before invading Normandy in the summer of 1449, the first stage in his clear intention of reuniting France.

Within a few weeks all of Normandy had been conquered by the French and the blame for the disaster was heaped squarely on the shoulders of Henry and his advisors. Lawless outbreaks of mob violence erupted across the country, resulting in the murder and execution of several of Henry's closest aides or advisors. At one stage a mob from Kent controlled by Jack Cade managed to enter London, seize control of the capital, and execute several noblemen. Henry fled northwards.

Pretending to listen to the rebels' grievances, Henry granted Cade a pardon, then turned on him and had him executed. To the opponents of the king – most of them supporters of the Duke of York – the dramatic about-turn was not clever management of the situation, but proof only of Henry's perfidy and inability to govern the realm. Soon they were appealing for York to return and save the kingdom from the utter disaster to which Henry and his counsellors would undoubtedly bring it.

As if answering a divine call to help save a country wrapped in confusion, Richard, Duke of York, decided to leave his post in Ireland and return to England. He landed in Anglesey, proclaiming that he had no personal ambitions for the throne and was interested only in the good of the country. Then he began to march towards Ludlow, adding soldiers to his retinue as he went.

Whatever his protestations, with Gloucester and Bedford now dead, the Duke of York – who, on both sides of his family, was descended from Edward III – had a powerful claim to the throne. As an alternative monarch to the weak and increasingly despised Henry VI he had assembled a legion of followers encouraging him to take action against Henry. The duke was not yet ready to take such a step, but there can be no doubt that his mind was already playing with the possibility of seizing the crown from Henry.

At the head of nearly 5,000 soldiers, York arrived in London on 29 September 1449 and there he confronted the king. He swore loyalty to Henry but insisted that his advisors, in particular his hated enemy the Duke of Somerset, would have to go. Henry refused and when, after frantic attempts to avoid armed conflict, Somerset was appointed commander of the town and garrison of Calais, it seemed as if York had missed his chance. He was forced to swear an oath of loyalty to Henry, declaring that any breach of this oath would be considered a matter of treason. He simmered with anger and resentment but, for the moment, acquiesced with the king's wishes.

Emboldened by his success Henry now presented his half-brothers, Edmund and Jasper Tudor, with earldoms. The two men had become important figures in the king's inner council and as a reward Edmund was made Earl of Richmond and Jasper Earl of Pembroke, titles that had previously been held by Henry's uncles, Bedford and Gloucester. Significantly, Edmund and Jasper were the first Welshmen ever to become peers of England, the start of a process of Anglicisation that would continue and consume ambitious Welshmen for several hundred years.

The Tudor boys were definitely going up in the world. When, in March 1453, Henry granted them joint wardship or custody of 9-year-old Margaret Beaufort, the daughter of one of his trusted advisors, it was another mark of the respect he held for his half-brothers. Wardship would invariably mutate into marriage at some stage and Henry was clearly telling the elder Tudor that it was time he settled down. Margaret was wealthy in her own right and that made it a beneficial alliance. As was expected, in the year 1455 Edmund married Margaret, despite her young age.

Marriage and the subsequent consummation must have been an ordeal for Margaret, a young girl barely into puberty. Edmund was twice her age, a brutal man schooled and experienced in the arts of war, but hardly the most caring and gentle of husbands and lovers. There was, however, method in his madness, as events were soon to show.

The marriage of Edmund and Margaret, and their acceptance by the king, was set in the face of a troubling period for England. Two years earlier a series of battles and sieges had marked the final moments of the Hundred Years War between England and France. The days of dynamic leadership had long gone and now the English armies in France were hindered by poor generals, inadequate supplies and equipment, and by French commanders who clearly knew what they were doing.

The last action was at Castillon where there was an overwhelming defeat for Henry's forces. It saw the English commander killed and his army scattered. The French had finally managed to push the English armies out of their country, a humiliating and irreversible setback for a nation that had once prided itself on its European territories.

There was worse to come. In August Henry VI, distraught at the defeat in France, suddenly collapsed in what was clearly a physical and emotional breakdown. He was unable to move or communicate and not even the news that his wife was pregnant could rouse him. Indeed, physical intimacy was an anathema to him and it is possible that the news simply increased his stress and actually contributed to his comatose condition.

Although news of the king's collapse was kept secret from the public at large, Henry's illness was a God-given second chance for the Duke of York. He was the most senior nobleman in the country and he now demanded to be appointed regent for the duration of the king's illness. Edmund Beaufort, the 2nd Duke of Somerset, and many of the nobles were opposed, but when Henry's wife Margaret threw her cap into the ring, expressing the view that power should rest with her, it was a step too far. The thought of a French princess exercising any sort of control over England was abhorrent and many noblemen, Edmund and Jasper Tudor among them, temporarily gave their support to the Duke of York.

With the king still in his catatonic state and armed supporters of the various nobles roaming the land, in March 1454 the Council finally realised they had little choice and appointed York to the position of Protector. The Duke of Somerset was sent to the Tower, Margaret 'exiled' to Windsor, and York began infiltrating his supporters into the Council.

Then, on Christmas Day 1454, the king made a sudden and surprising recovery. He had no knowledge of what had happened during his time in what was really a coma but, once out of the trance he seemed to recover his sensibilities and decision-making powers. Almost immediately he dismissed York as Protector and released Somerset from the Tower. York hurriedly left London, without any formal farewells – effectively an insult to the king – knowing that Somerset would now be out for his blood.

Henry and Somerset were soon hot on his heels, leaving the city at the beginning of May 1455. York was waiting for them at St Albans, his soldiers drawn up for battle and demanding that Somerset be handed over to him. Soon street fighting broke out in the town, York's troops pursuing the king's fleeing forces through the narrow alleyways. Henry was wounded in the neck and captured. On York's orders he was taken to the abbey for safety.

Somerset, realising that the situation was now desperate, barricaded himself into an inn, along with his few remaining followers, but York's men simply battered down the door. Knowing that his fate was sealed the Duke of Somerset charged across the room towards his enemy, but was hacked down by the battle axes and swords of the Yorkists. It was a brutal end for Somerset but one that York certainly enjoyed.

Jasper Tudor had been present at the battle – rout would be a more accurate word – but had been able to do little to stop the catastrophe. He accompanied the captive king when York now marched him back to London.

Surprisingly, neither of the Tudors lost their lands or titles, a fate that befell many of the king's supporters in the wake of York's victory. Richard of York could clearly see the benefits of befriending the brothers and keeping them on his side. Things did not go so well for Henry, however. Not surprisingly, following his defeat he suffered another breakdown and now the Tudors found themselves in a difficult position.

They were obviously loyal to their half-brother. He, after all, had granted them titles and estates, had made them the men they now were. But they were realistic enough to see that things could not continue like this for very long. They had a degree of sympathy for York and his party but they remained solidly Lancastrian at heart.

The Duke of York was again appointed Protector, the position lasting until February 1456 when Henry made yet another remarkable recovery and took up the reins of leadership again. Despite keeping York close at hand as an advisor, it was clear to everyone that the real power now lay not with the king, but with his driven and, some would say, deadly wife. Queen Margaret hated York and was determined to destroy his influence and, if necessary, the man himself.

X X X

Even with Henry 'recovered' there remained an atmosphere of latent hostility both in the court and in the country and the two Tudors found themselves in direct opposition to the Duke of York. In his stronghold at Carmarthen, Edmund was soon under attack by Yorkist forces. Outnumbered and with provisions running low things began to look increasingly bleak for Edmund Tudor.

When Carmarthen Castle was finally taken Edmund was imprisoned in his own fortress. It was a period of custody that did not last long. On 1 November 1456 he died, probably from plague contracted while in prison.

On Edmund's death his wife Margaret, the tiny 13-year-old bride, was sent further west, to Pembroke, for her own safety. She was seven months pregnant when she arrived at Jasper's fortress and there was a clear need to keep her safe from the Yorkist forces.

13

However, it was the fear of her contracting the plague which had killed her husband that was the main reason for sending her westwards. From the moment she had conceived, Edmund had always known that Margaret had to live long enough to give birth to what he hoped was a son. Then, as Earl of Richmond, the child would inherit the Tudor estates and so preserve the line – his main reason for taking such a young and seemingly vulnerable girl as a wife and for making her pregnant.

Meanwhile tensions between the Yorkists and the Lancastrian party of the king and queen continued to bubble and boil. On many occasions those tensions erupted into physical violence, small skirmishes and larger pitched battles marking the decade. A Lancastrian army led by Queen Margaret was defeated at Blore Heath in September 1459, but a month later, outside Ludlow, York's troops refused to fight against their king, leaving Margaret and Henry in possession of the field.

It was a significant setback for York and his supporters who had always prided themselves on filling the role of the popul:rist party. They had gleefully presented themselves as nobles, yes, but with the needs of the people at the forefront of all their minds, deeds and actions. The duke and his youngest son Edmund were forced to flee into Wales while York's eldest boy, Edward, fled to Calais.

Determined to exploit her victory, Margaret summoned a Parliament to meet at Coventry and in an Act of Attainder passed by what became known as the 'Parliament of Devils', the Duke of York, his eldest son and nearly thirty nobles were stripped of their titles. The Tudors were some of the beneficiaries, Jasper being granted the lordship of Denbeigh and his father Owen being given an annuity of £100.

Realising that if he wanted to be safe he needed to put distance between himself and Queen Margaret, the Duke of York took ship and established himself in Ireland. England, however, remained his main goal.

Broadsheets and open letters continually bombarded the country, enforcing the view that York and his supporters were the 'men of the people', and that the king had been led astray by evil followers. It was a propaganda campaign that seemed to be working as discontent with Henry and Margaret, who now appeared to have decamped to the Midlands, grew steadily. The citizens of London, in particular, resented the move out of the capital and felt abandoned by the king.

On 26 June 1460 York's eldest son Edward, accompanied by his powerful friend Richard Neville, the 16th Earl of Warwick returned to the fray, landing unopposed in Kent. Accompanied by 2,000 men-at-arms they marched northwards, hundreds of supporters and soldiers joining them as they went. Canterbury threw open its gates but Edward paused only briefly before marching on to London. Here he was again welcomed with open arms. His real target, however, was Northampton where the Lancastrians had set up camp. Soon the two armies were facing each other across the open summer fields.

The battle lasted just half an hour and resulted in total victory for the Yorkists. Henry was captured and taken back to London while Margaret fled to Wales where she sought refuge in Jasper's castle at Harlech. When the Duke of York received news of the victory and finally took ship from Ireland it was clear that he came not as a loyal supporter of the king, but as an alternative monarch.

However, while he was enthusiastically received by the people, the nobles of the land refused to give the duke their support to take the throne. The most they would do was to push an Act through Parliament which formally recognised York as Henry's heir. Queen Margaret, now in Scotland, was furious; as far as she was concerned there was but one heir to the throne, her son. She quickly assembled an army and marched south to confront the Yorkist pretender.

The two forces came face to face outside Wakefield on a bleak and freezing winter day. To begin with there was little attempt at battle, but late in the afternoon of 30 December 1460, in a foolhardy gamble, York led a body of troops out of Sandal Castle and charged the Lancastrian line. He was isolated, dragged from his horse and killed. His son Edmund also died in the charge. The treatment meted out to York's body clearly shows the anger and the hatred of the time. His corpse was propped up on an ant heap, a paper crown upon his head while the Lancastrian soldiers filed past hurling insults at the dead man:-

> Hail King, without rule. Hail King, without ancestry. Hail leader and Prince with no subjects or possessions.
> (John Whethamstede, Abbot of
> St Albans, quoted in Skidmore, p.41)

Despite the death of the Duke of York the conflict continued. The brutality and bloodshed displayed by both sides meant that forgiveness was the last thing on anyone's mind. Ambition and hatred; it was a lethal combination.

Edward, now the eldest surviving son of the duke, gained revenge for his father's death when, at Mortimer's Cross on 2 February 1461, he skilfully defeated and then massacred a force led by the Earl of Wiltshire and Jasper Tudor. Over 4,000 Lancastrians, many of them Welshmen in the service of Jasper, were killed. Among the casualties was Owen Tudor who was captured, taken to Hereford and executed just after the battle.

Jasper fled to his castle at Pembroke, vowing vengeance on Edward and all of the Yorkists for the death of his father. Revenge was one thing, but his main job now was to protect the life of his young nephew, a 4-year-old boy playing happily and innocently within the confines of the castle walls. He was one of the last surviving Lancastrian princes, after the king and his son, and from now on Jasper would dedicate his life to the task of keeping him safe.

Meanwhile the disputes and conflict between the noblemen of England continued, becoming bloodier and more violent with each engagement or battle. In 1461 a Lancastrian victory at St Albans resulted in Margaret once again 'taking possession' of the king, but this was offset when, on 4 March 1461, the nobles and clergy of the country proclaimed Edward, Earl of March and son of the Duke of York, as King Edward IV.

With Henry VI, his wife and son still on the loose, Edward knew that there had to be one final showdown if his claim to the throne was to have any substance. The Battle of Towton was fought on 29 March 1461, Palm Sunday, in a bleak and bitter snowstorm. It has been estimated that as many as 50,000 men joined in the combat with over 28,000 becoming casualties. It was the bloodiest battle in English history and resulted in complete victory for Edward and his Yorkist forces.

Henry, Margaret and their son Edward fled into Scotland, but although the Lancastrian cause was severely damaged it was not broken. As long as Queen Margaret had life in her body she would continue to fight for the House of Lancaster and, in particular, for her husband and son.

The ever ambitious and energetic queen was soon engaged in negotiations with Louis XI, the new French king, and it was not long before she and 800 French troops were ensconced at Bamburgh Castle on the coast of northern England. There Henry joined her. Jasper Tudor was also present but the Lancastrians were outnumbered and on Christmas Eve 1461 Bamburgh surrendered. Now Jasper's castle at Harlech became almost the final centre of support for King Henry.

Hopes of further help from Louis were dashed when a treaty was signed between him and Edward, promising friendship and mutual cooperation. Some assistance was found in the shape of the Duke of Brittany but it was limited and of little real value. When Lancastrian forces were defeated at Hexham on 15 May 1461 it was almost the end.

Wales remained the one real bastion of Lancastrian support, mainly due to the efforts of Jasper Tudor. He continued to campaign in North Wales, capturing the town of Denbeigh and putting the county of Flintshire to the sword. On 14 August, however, Lord Herbert managed to force Harlech to surrender and, in despair, Jasper took ship to Brittany.

With the war seemingly won Edward now turned to what he, rather naively, thought were more pleasant matters. He courted and married Elizabeth Woodville. Never before had an English monarch married for love and the diplomats in his court were appalled by an action that left their plans of foreign alliances high and dry.

The Woodvilles were not of royal blood but members of the clan, men like Anthony Woodville and John Grey, were ambitious and unpopular and it was an alliance that effectively split the nobility of the country in half. Rumours of sorcery and witchcraft ran rife – how else could the Woodvilles have gained control over the new king?

More importantly, the marriage lost Edward the support of his great ally and friend Richard Neville, the Earl of Warwick. Known as Warwick the Kingmaker, his influence at court, and in the country at large, was vast. Warwick was a schemer whose name 'Kingmaker' was an appellation well bestowed and he had his own ideas for Edward's future. He had his eye on potential allies and was in the process of arranging a political marriage for Edward, with a French princess. His plans did certainly not include marriage to a commoner.

Something had to give. In 1470, after a confused and increasingly bitter period of argument and negotiation, Warwick felt that he had no option but to flee the country and take refuge in France. The Yorkist star was dimmed but, for the moment, it seemed as if Edward, despite the opposition of Warwick, had managed to retain power.

As ever during the Wars of the Roses, fortunes soon swung the other way. Warwick gathered together an army, invaded England and, after victory at the Battle of Edgecote, forced King Edward IV to flee. It was an amazing turn around with the hunter now the hunted. Edward took ship for Flanders accompanied by his younger brother Richard, Duke of Gloucester, leaving Warwick in control of the country.

Henry was released from the Tower and reinstated as king. However, his already fragile mental health was further damaged by the simple fact that Warwick, until now a mortal enemy and supporter of Edward, was the very man who had brought him back to the throne. He was confused and unsure, wondering what might happen next.

Henry's reinstatement, his readeption as it was known, did not last long. In 1471 Edward returned from his exile, out-manoeuvred Warwick in a series of tactical marches and entered London in triumph. He was reunited with his wife, who had spent the period of Edward's exile in sanctuary at Westminster Abbey, and the unfortunate Henry was once again locked up in the Tower.

Edward now went to war on Warwick the Kingmaker and on the last of the Lancastrians. Firstly, on a field shrouded by fog and mist, he defeated Warwick's army at the Battle of Barnet. It was a confused affair with the artillery of the Earl of Warwick managing to fire all night on what they thought was the enemy when in reality they were overshooting the mark by huge distances.

Edward's best and most sensible decision during that noisy but ineffective night was to stop his own artillery firing back and thus giving away their true position. The battle began the following morning and was over almost before it was light. Warwick, realising that the situation was desperate, tried to run from the field, find his horse and escape. He was bludgeoned to his knees; his visor was torn open and Warwick the Kingmaker was knifed to death. (Article: *History Revealed*, p.47)

After his victory at Barnet, Edward proceeded to eliminate the last significant Lancastrian resistance at the Battle of Tewkesbury. It was one of the final but also one of the most vicious battles of the Wars of the Roses. Edward knew that this was the one encounter he could not afford to lose and, as a consequence, made it clear that the enemy was to be ruthlessly hunted down and eliminated.

With Richard of Gloucester in the van, the fighting at Tewkesbury spilled over from what is still referred to in the area as 'Bloody Meadow', into the lanes leading down to the river and into the streets of the town. It even extended into the abbey itself as the vanquished Lancastrians tried desperately to find sanctuary. Their attempts were doomed to failure as there was no quarter given and even the house of God became a battlefield. There was apparently so much blood shed in the aisles and chapels of the abbey that the place had to be re-sanctified in the days and weeks after the battle.

The 17-year-old Edward, Prince of Wales, was killed during the battle, cut down and ruthlessly despatched like so many other Lancastrians. As the Crowland Chronicle, a continuous account of English history compiled by the monks of Crowland Abbey, rather discretely puts it, his life was ended by 'avenging hands'.

The death of the Prince of Wales came as his mother Margaret watched helplessly from the tower of Tewkesbury Abbey. With defeat apparent, Queen Margaret fled to a religious house not far away in the Malvern Hills. She was discovered by Edward's troops a week later and imprisoned in London.

Held in captivity for several years Margaret was later returned to France where, without power or influence, she died in 1482. It was a sad and ignominious end for a woman who had been the centre of politics in England for so many years.

A few days after the Battle of Tewkesbury Henry VI also met his end in the Tower of London. It had been a long time coming but now, after hovering between life and death, success and failure for so long, the true King of England was dead.

To begin with the causes of Henry's death were not clear, one account stating that he died from 'melancholy'. Given his emotional state such an end was quite possible – indeed, with all of the ups and downs he had suffered since ascending the throne, his numerous moments of power followed by inevitable falling from grace, it was a miracle he had survived so long.

A slight, inept man, he was saintly rather than worldly wise, really little more than a puppet for people like his wife Margaret and, to an extent, Warwick the Kingmaker. They could control and direct him, something Henry found difficult to do for himself.

Henry should never, really, have been king. Perhaps if his father had lived longer he might have matured more fully under his shadow, or at least been trained in the arts of kingship. But coming to the throne at the age of just 9 months there were expectations placed upon him from an early age, expectations with which he was not able to cope.

The great misfortune of Henry VI was that he was in the wrong place at the wrong time, when there were many more ruthless and ambitious opponents around. So, to begin with, people were happy to accept the notion that he had died from emotional strain or stress.

However, things were not always what they seemed. People might have wanted to believe that the king had just wasted away; that was a fairly gentle, easily accepted version of his death that did not trouble the imagination or the conscience. Reality, however, was somewhat different.

It later emerged that Henry's death came after a blow with a heavy object, perhaps a hammer or a lance, to the back of the head. The identity of the killer or killers remains unknown but it is highly likely that the engineer behind the murder was the new sovereign, Edward IV.

Edward, with the memory of Warwick's recent switch of alliances still vivid in his mind, had had enough. From now on he would take no more chances and two kings of England, even if one was simple-minded and in captivity, was one monarch too many.

Edward may have thought that killing Henry would finally put an end to the dynastic wars that had blighted England for years. If he had only known – his actions had done little more than unleash the final stages of the Wars of the Roses.

Chapter Three

Birth, Adolescence and Exile

This, then, was the world into which Henry Tudor, Earl of Richmond, was born. It was a lawless time, one of bloodthirsty battles, perpetual warfare, murder and mayhem. Life expectancy was limited: men, women and children regularly and ruthlessly cut down either by disease or through battle. Even someone like Henry Tudor was as vulnerable and as liable to meet a sudden end as the lowest archer in the service of his Uncle Jasper.

Little is known about the early life of Henry Tudor. Even the exact place of his birth is open to debate and discussion. The massive bulk of Pembroke Castle at the far end of Wales was undoubtedly the location. It was – and remains – a magnificent fortress, standing at the end of a long narrow promontory or ridge flanked by two valleys that in the fifteenth century were tidal inlets:-

> The extreme western end of the ridge gathers itself into a rocky limestone headland, rather like a clenched fist at the end of a knotty, sinewy arm. On this rugged outcrop with its soaring, almost perpendicular cliffs, stands Pembroke Castle.
> (Carradice: *Pembroke: For King and Parliament* p.9)

So, Pembroke Castle, yes, the fact is incontrovertible. But the specific part of that castle where the event took place remains unclear.

It has been suggested that the place of Henry's birth might have been a small room at the eastern end of the great Northern Hall in the castle. It was not really a separate room, just a chamber that was partitioned off from the rest of the room.

That would be possible but Margaret Beaufort was by then a countess, despite her young age, and it is unlikely that her confinement and the delivery of her son would have taken place in what was really little more than an annex to a public area of the fortress. Nobles, guards, even common soldiers and washer women had direct and easy access to the Hall at all times of the day and night. That makes the suggestion highly unlikely.

Another suggestion is a room above the main Gate House, the huge and imposing barrier that still stands like a sentinel guarding the entrance to the castle. This is more likely than a room off the Northern Hall; the Gate House was, after all, a fortress in itself and if one of the aims of sending Margaret to Pembroke was to keep her safe then the Gate House was as secure as anywhere.

The Gate House, however, was potentially one of the first places that any assaulting army would attack. It sat on the southern wall of the castle and with the fortress at nearby Carmarthen having recently fallen to the Yorkists, it is unlikely that Jasper would have risked the life of his brother's wife by placing her in such an exposed position. The Gate House might well have been suggested as the place of birth but no one has yet identified, or even hazarded a guess at, a possible chamber within the building where it might have occurred.

The third possibility – and the one which is now commonly accepted – is a room on the first floor of what is called the Henry VII Tower. The tower sits on the southern wall to the immediate right of the Gate House and like most of the towers in the castle it extends over several floors.

The rationale behind this choice is the chimney breast in the room which bears the remains of Henry's coat of arms. The decoration had at one time been let into the wall above the fireplace. There is no date for the embellishment but it is clearly old. This appears to fit with the words of antiquarian and writer John Leland who visited the castle during his tour of the country in 1538. He wrote that he had seen:-

> The chamber where King Henri VII was born, in knowledge whereof a chymeney is new made with the armes and badges of King Henri.
>
> (Leland: *De Uris Illustribus* / *On Famous Men* no page number/reference)

The coat of arms is there, or at least the remains of it, but such an embellishment could easily have adorned several other bed chambers in the castle. None have been found, but decorations in other rooms might have existed and been destroyed over the years – particularly after Oliver Cromwell took the fortress in 1648. He ordered the place to be slighted and the Puritan soldiers, with little liking for royal emblems, went about their work with a will.

The Tower, like the Gate House, lies on the outside wall and is, arguably, even more exposed to attack. It is relatively small and hardly becoming for one of the most significant occupants of the castle. Leland was operating on the instructions of Thomas Cromwell, chief minister to Henry VIII, son of Harri Tudor. It had been 'suggested' to him that he might find an appropriate chamber and, therefore, he may well have had a vested interest in identifying a place of birth for his paymaster and for the king.

At the end of the day it is all surmise. Henry was born in Pembroke Castle in the year 1457 but the location of the exact room where he first entered the world will probably never be fully established.

X X X

Two months after giving birth to her son, Margaret Beaufort left the safety of Pembroke Castle and headed east. She was accompanied by Jasper Tudor who had returned from Brittany with the express intention of making her and his infant nephew totally safe. To do that, he knew, Margaret would have to take a new husband, someone who would protect her and prevent the king – whoever he might be – parcelling her off to whichever nobleman he felt most appropriate.

Jasper already had someone in mind. It was the sole reason he was taking what might otherwise be regarded as a hazardous and dangerous journey to the Newport area of eastern Wales. The wealthy and powerful Duke of Buckingham was keen to find a wife for his second son, Henry Stafford, and Margaret fitted the bill perfectly. The match was duly made and Margaret and Stafford were married at the beginning of 1458.

The young Henry was left behind at Pembroke in the care of his nurse. She was a Welsh woman, the wife of Philip ap Howell of Carmarthen. Her name remains unknown but it is more than probable that she had accompanied Margaret Beaufort when, as a pregnant and frightened girl, the countess had left the home of her husband Edmund. The nurse spoke Welsh and might even have taught the young Henry to speak a few words of her language. It is doubtful if he maintained his Welsh but, even so, he remained very fond of his nurse and after coming to the throne awarded her a pension.

As the Wars of the Roses ground on, times of open warfare contrasting with months of troubled and uneasy peace, Henry Tudor – now recognised in the eyes of everyone as the Earl of Richmond – grew from baby to toddler to little boy in the safety of Pembroke Castle. With his nurse he would have walked or ridden along the banks of the Pembroke River or even sailed out into the broad reaches of Milford Haven. He would have begun learning the arts of war, even at his young age, playing with wooden swords and bows and arrows in the castle courtyard.

He was a thoughtful child who loved stories and tales of great deeds. He might have missed his mother but his nurse was always there and Pembroke Castle would have been a solidly reassuring bastion around his tiny body. His Uncle Jasper came and went but young Henry knew that he was working for the Lancastrian cause and that his support and friendship could always be counted on.

And then things changed. After their calamitous defeat at Towton the Lancastrian forces were in disarray but Jasper Tudor still remained in control of much of Wales. In an effort to end this threat, in 1461 Edward IV ordered Lord Herbert to reclaim the country for the Yorkists. In particular he was to seize Jasper's stronghold at Pembroke.

The castle fell on 30 September, surrendering through lack of provisions and supplies rather than being taken by storm. Jasper was not present when the castle capitulated, a fact that probably contributed to Herbert's easy success. But more important than simply capturing the castle, the Yorkists also now had possession of one of the most significant people in the realm – the 5-year-old Henry Tudor, the last hope of the Lancastrian cause.

Jasper was soon stripped of his titles by Edward and once again went into exile. His aim, however, remained true – he wanted to keep his nephew safe, even though the boy was now in Yorkist hands, and he dreamed a constant dream of restoring the House of Lancaster to the throne. In his life he spent long periods abroad, in exile, but returned to England several times. He was, however, invariably on the losing side in the battles against Edward. The only real succour came in the form of support and friendship from the Duke of Brittany. In the years ahead that would be a very important factor for both Jasper and his nephew.

As for Henry, the young man was placed into the custody of Lord William Herbert, the very man who had taken Pembroke Castle from his Uncle Jasper. In 1462 Herbert was granted the wardship of Henry, hoping to eventually marry him off to one of his daughters. Based at the recently refurbished Raglan Castle in Monmouthshire, the boy was well looked after by Herbert's wife Anne – he was, after all, a potential son-in-law – and, of course, the ever-faithful Welsh nurse was still there, at least for the next few years.

It was at Raglan that Henry matured and developed into adolescence. He learned quickly, remarkably quickly, excelling at his books and in the techniques of archery and swordsmanship. Practice was one thing, however; the reality of the battlefield was something entirely different – as Henry was about to find out.

In 1469, when Warwick the Kingmaker returned to challenge the king after his brief period of exile, Edward ordered Lord Herbert to join him in the coming conflict and Herbert duly left Raglan Castle at the head of a large body of infantry. Riding with him was the 12-year-old Henry Tudor, eager to witness and maybe even take part in his first battle.

The Battle of Edgecote was yet another bloody clash which left Warwick as the victor – and now it was Edward's turn to flee. Lord Herbert was captured and, when the fighting was over, beheaded. The king's forces were scattered across the countryside.

Henry sat astride his horse watching the carnage and devastation on the field of battle. He was eventually led from the field and took refuge at the house of Lord Ferrers, the brother of Herbert's widow, in Herefordshire. There he recovered from his ordeal and, in the words of Chris Skidmore, 'soon returned to his archery practice'. (Skidmore: *Bosworth, the Birth of the Tudors* Page 62)

The death of Lord Herbert had freed Henry from his wardship and now, with his mother – with whom he had maintained regular but distant contact all of the time he was in the care of the Herberts – petitioning for a return of all his lands and estates, the boy was happy to remain with Lord Ferrers in Herefordshire.

Contact between Henry and his mother increased greatly in these months; it was a pleasurable time for both of them. Following the return of Henry VI to the throne in 1470 Margaret Beaufort and Jasper decided that young Harri, now 13 years old, should meet with the king and make a personal appeal for the return of his estates.

The meeting duly took place. Quite what the two individuals, one a boy of just 13, the other not really in tune with his own thoughts, let alone anyone else's, felt about each other is not known. It must have been a puzzling occasion, especially for the king.

Lancastrian legend states that at this meeting and at a series of further contacts between the two men, Henry VI was much impressed by Harri and even promised the throne to the young Tudor earl. Feeble as the king might be, such a gift or promise was highly unlikely, but Tudor propagandists, desperate for any morsel that could be added to their man's claim to the throne, took and used the story as the gospel truth.

In November 1470 Henry and Jasper left London and rode back into Wales. Henry had enjoyed his time with his mother, bonding with her in a way he had never been allowed to do before. But the situation in the country was still delicately poised and Jasper knew that Henry would be safer and more secure well away from the capital.

There is no record of how Henry felt about returning to his childhood home. But with Henry established securely and safely at Pembroke, at least Jasper could now afford to sit back and reflect on the situation.

Quite apart from the love he had for the boy, he could see that Henry had become the final hope of the House of Lancaster. With Henry VI and his son both dead everything now rested on the shoulders of the young Earl of Richmond. Jasper knew that – and, more importantly, he knew that King Edward also knew it.

Following his crushing victory at Tewkesbury in May 1471 Edward finally felt secure on the throne. He had eliminated almost all of the potential threats – Henry VI, Edward the Prince of Wales and Henry's heir, the Earl of Warwick and, indeed, nearly all of his obvious enemies. Only Jasper Tudor and his nephew remained at large, holed up in Pembroke Castle. Morgan ap Thomas, a relative of Henry's later ally Rhys ap Thomas, was despatched by Edward with orders to capture the castle and take the two Tudors into custody.

It was never going to be an easy task. Jasper had fully provisioned his fortress and the mighty walls were lined with soldiers. Morgan quickly realised he had no chance of battering his way into the castle and instead decided to 'dig in' and begin a siege.

Whether the castle would have been starved into submission will never be known. Just a week after the siege lines had been drawn, trenches and saps constructed, Dafydd, the brother of Morgan ap Thomas, arrived on the scene with what has been recorded as 'a peasant army'. As in any civil war the two brothers supported different sides in the conflict and Dafydd immediately attacked and dispersed Morgan's troops.

It was a brief respite as stronger forces under Lord Ferrers had already been despatched by the king, but it gave Jasper and Henry the opportunity they needed to escape the bottleneck that Pembroke Castle had become. To flee the country now seemed to Jasper to be the only way to keep Henry safe. He had used flight as a means of keeping safe – as had the king – on several occasions and so he took the opportunity presented to him by the dispute between the two Thomas brothers.

As soon as they could, Jasper and Henry left Pembroke Castle and, together with a number of servants and helpers, headed for the nearby town and port of Tenby. Included in the party was a Pembrokeshire soldier by the name of Arnold Butler, a man who would later feature quite significantly in the story of Henry Tudor and his subsequent march to Bosworth Field.

It would have been a perilous journey from Pembroke to Tenby as the forces of Morgan ap Thomas were still in the area and on the lookout for anyone escaping or leaving the castle. The escape was probably done by night and with the need to maintain secrecy there would have been no torches to light the way. It would have been a case of horses slowly and carefully picking their way across broken ground, everyone trusting to luck and praying that there would be no stumble or fall which would have led only to broken legs and disaster.

Jasper and Henry made the trip successfully, however, and soon arrived in Tenby. The town was just 12 miles to the east of Pembroke and, in those days, was still an important trading port. Ships and coasters would be coming and going almost every day with trade links well established with places like France and Spain. It was a cosmopolitan and busy environment where foreign visitors, exotically dressed sailors and strangers were commonplace and well treated by the population.

Jasper was already familiar with the place, having been instrumental in strengthening the town walls in 1457. Under his direction the walls had been widened to 6ft, and a dry ditch that ran around the landward sides of the town was greatly extended. It made the town far more defendable but Jasper had no intention of sitting there to be attacked.

The town mayor, Thomas White, had worked with Jasper during these modifications and remained a personal friend. It was this man who would now offer help to the fleeing Tudors, giving them sanctuary in his imposing town house.

And here, once again, truth begins to mingle and mix with legend. According to the story Jasper and Henry were hidden in the cellar of

Thomas White in the main street of the town (now Tudor Square) before escaping down a tunnel that led to the harbour.

A tunnel to the harbour which lay a quarter of a mile away would have been unlikely and unnecessary. Thomas White's house (now Boots the Chemist) stood high up on the cliff above the bay and any tunnel would have to drop at least a 100ft before it reached the level of the harbour. Digging such a tunnel in the rock and descending such a steep slope would have been almost impossible, whoever was charged to construct it. One thing is clear: Jasper and Henry had neither the time nor the inclination to dig such a structure. If there was a tunnel it had been dug there many years before.

There was undoubtedly a cavern under the house, used for storage, and here Jasper and Henry could well have stayed for a brief period. Many of the houses in the main street of Tenby had such facilities – the place was, after all, a trading centre of some repute. Local legend states that a warren of tunnels stretched between many of the houses in the town, but if this is true they would have been short and not requiring a drop of many, many feet.

Thomas White's cavern or store house would probably have had a rear entrance, a highly necessary facility. Through this rear entrance workers would have been able to bring in barrels and other goods that White's business enterprises demanded without having to go around to the front door. But a tunnel that reached all the way down to the harbour seems highly unlikely.

Apart from anything else, at this stage in proceedings there was no need to use a tunnel as the troops of Lord Ferrers, sent by Edward, had not yet reached Tenby. Caution was certainly required but total secrecy was not really needed.

How long the Tudor earls stayed with White is not known, but with Yorkist forces inching closer by the day it could not have been long. Jasper would not have wanted to incriminate his friend who, after all, would be staying behind. Thomas White had the use of several ships so the means of escaping from Tenby was already there. It was just a matter of choosing the best time when the wind and tide were in their favour.

Rather than use the mythical tunnel it is more likely that under the cover of darkness the Tudors simply went out of the cavern by the back way and followed the alleyways and narrow lanes down to the harbour.

There they boarded a barque belonging to Thomas White and set sail for France on 2 June 1471.

It was Henry's first taste of exile, hardly an enthralling thought, but the flight and the sense of fear, the exquisite feeling of tension that accompanies almost any nefarious activity, would have appealed to his adventurous spirit. He did not know it at this stage, but he would remain in exile for the next fourteen years.

Chapter Four

Brittany and Home Again

When Jasper and Henry Tudor left Tenby in June 1471 they were intending to make landfall in France. Jasper had previously enjoyed the hospitality of Louis XI, his cousin, and had even been awarded a pension by the French king. Apart from family ties, which were admittedly not always reliable and were open to change at any given moment, Louis was a natural enemy of Edward and the Yorkists. It was this factor rather than the family connection that made Louis a potential ally. As Jasper explained to Henry, he expected that they would be well received at the French court.

Unfortunately for Jasper and Henry, their ship was hit by severe storms and blown off course. The young Henry probably suffered from sea sickness; Jasper, well used to scurrying back and forth across the Channel, would have endured the vagaries of the weather much better.

The 'running men' sought a brief respite in Jersey, pleased to be off the rocking, rolling barque, at least for a while. Then they boarded her . again and set out once more for France. The weather was no better and when they next came ashore it was at the tiny port of La Conquet near Brest. Far from making landfall in France they found themselves in the duchy of Brittany.

News of their landing was quickly relayed to the Duke of Brittany, Francis II. The duke was perfectly happy to greet the unexpected arrivals and despatched soldiers to bring them to his palace in Vannes. Jasper was more than willing to throw himself and Henry onto the mercy of Duke Francis, who was a charitable man. He was also, however, a pragmatic ruler. He would offer the pair sanctuary, all the while knowing that the Tudors could be very useful to him in the three-way diplomatic game between Brittany, France and England.

Edward was furious when he learned that the two Tudors had escaped from Pembroke and even offered financial incentives to get Francis to send them back to England. It was an unsuccessful ploy as Francis knew only too well the value of the two refugees. He was determined to keep them in Brittany and, although the Tudors were given all of the grace and favour of distinguished visitors, they were still closely guarded. It was a genteel captivity, as much to prevent them escaping as it was to stop any attempted kidnapping by Edward's agents.

Meanwhile Henry's mother, Margaret Beaufort, had taken a third husband. He was Lord Thomas Stanley, one of the richest men in the country and, at this stage, a confirmed supporter of Edward IV and the Yorkists. It seemed that Margaret, like many of the Lancastrian elite, was now hitching her star to the Yorkist cause. If she was indeed changing her allegiance it was with one aim in mind – a pardon for her son and the reclaiming of the estates due to him as the Earl of Richmond.

Henry spent a large number of his exile years at the castle of Suscinio, a fairly luxurious residence that was traditionally the summer palace of Duke Francis. The castle, however, was more of a chateau than a fortress and lay in an exposed position, open to attack from the sea. It meant that Henry and Jasper were often on the move, travelling either alone or with the duke's court between palaces and castles in towns like Vannes, Nantes and Rennes.

Despite the surveillance from the duke's guards the next few years were a relatively pleasant time for the young man who filled his days with reading and riding in the countryside. In the evenings he was like any other courtier, impressing everyone with his good looks and his manners. He knew that he was, really, a prisoner but was determined to enjoy this genteel captivity as best he could.

Edward kept up his efforts to have the Tudors returned to England, even suggesting to Margaret Beaufort that he would be prepared to marry off his daughter Elizabeth to her young son. Such a move would have effectively wiped out the twin threat of both Lancaster and the Tudors, but in the end the suggestion came to nothing.

Edward may have been genuine in his expressed desire to unite the Houses of York and Lancaster, or he may well have had more sinister intentions in laying his hands on Henry. Whatever he wanted to do he was thwarted by Francis who always held the whip hand – if Edward would help him to maintain the independence of Brittany from France, the duke hinted, he would certainly consider returning the Earl of Richmond. And one day that nearly happened.

By 1476 Duke Francis was ill and worn down by the continual pressure from both England and France to send the Tudors packing. Louis had already granted Jasper a pension of over £1,000 and therefore considered him his liege man – his place was not in Brittany but in Paris! Sick and not thinking clearly, under this pressure from both Louis and Edward, Francis eventually agreed to send Henry back to England.

Henry seemed to have no option but to go along with the decision. However, at the port of St Malo, prior to sailing, he developed a sudden illness. It may have been a faked attack, it may have been genuine, but his collapse delayed the sailing and then caused it to be cancelled. After a few days Henry simply turned around and returned to the duke's court where he was enthusiastically received by everyone, including a revived and rejuvenated Francis. He was, after all, a very handsome young man who was always welcome at court.

X X X

Edward IV died, suddenly and unexpectedly, on 4 April 1483. His reign had been punctuated by bouts of lethargy and disinterest on his part but there was no doubt that he had given England a much-needed period of calm. Now everything seemed to be up in the air again.

Edward was succeeded by his son Edward V, but as a boy of just 12 the new king was regarded as a minor and control of the country passed into the hands of a Royal Council of noblemen. Prominent among these great nobles were Lord William Hastings, formerly Chancellor for Edward IV, and the brother of Edward, Richard, Duke of Gloucester. Richard's behaviour and attitudes were already beginning to take on sinister proportions but what happened next was swift and deadly.

On the orders of Richard, the young King Edward V was taken to London where he and his 9-year-old brother were lodged in the Tower – for their own safety, as Richard had it. They never emerged again and the legend of the 'Princes in the Tower' was born.

Hastings, Richard's chief rival in the Council, was betrayed and set up by William Catesby, one of Richard's agents and paid men who had as much to gain out of 'fingering' Hastings as Richard himself. Hastings, accused of treason, was the last real impediment to Richard's ambitions and he found himself arrested and convicted without the benefit of trial He was executed – over a log rather than the traditional block – on 13 June 1483.

Then it was time to deal with the hated Woodvilles. Anthony Woodville and Richard Grey of the Woodville family were apprehended and executed, again without trial, and on 22 June the marriage of Edward IV and Elizabeth Woodville was declared illegal. It meant that the two sons from the marriage, Edward V and Richard of Shrewsbury, were illegitimate and therefore debarred from the throne. On 26 June 1483 Richard of Gloucester was declared King Richard III. As the Crowland Chronicle had it 'In the great hall of Westminster he thrust himself into the marble chair.' (The Crowland Chronicle, 1486)

The motives behind Richard's seizure of power have been debated for years. Ambition and a desire for power – Polydore Vergil called it 'An ardent desire of soveraigntie' (Vergil, Book 25) – were at the root and while many at the time regarded his coup as a necessary evil to stop a recurrence of the Wars of the Roses, there were others who objected – and objected violently.

That summer there was a major rebellion against the new king, undoubtedly fostered and designed by Margaret Beaufort who was clear that her son Henry was the only rightful heir to the throne of England. Margaret was just one of many powerful women in England during the Wars of the Roses. Along with people like Catherine de Valois, Margaret of Anjou and her son's future wife, Elizabeth of York, Margaret Beaufort was dynamic, energetic and undoubtedly highly devious. She seemed to be at the forefront of almost every scheme or plan to advance her particular cause and never shied away from taking the unpopular decision.

Henry, still waiting in Brittany, was given an important part to play in the rebellion. A series of uprisings were planned to take place in several different parts of the country. These would be supported by the Duke of Buckingham who would march from his base in Wales, and by Henry Tudor who would come by sea from Brittany. Unfortunately for the rebels their plans were ruined by bad weather and bad timing.

The uprising in Kent took place ten days too soon and Richard had more than enough time to muster an army, march out from London and crush the rebels. He was a fine soldier and the rebels, most of them just peasants and country folk, had no chance against his superior generalship.

Informers and spies had warned Richard that Buckingham, previously a staunch friend and supporter of the king, had changed his allegiance and was soon to march into England. Buckingham's motives remain unclear as he had been in great favour with Richard and may even have played a part in the murder of the Princes in the Tower. If that was true he knew that such a deed could well come back to haunt him.

Buckingham also had distant links to the long-dead Edward III and may, therefore, have had his own designs on the throne. Or perhaps he believed that Richard had only a tenuous hold on the crown and would take others – Buckingham in particular – down with him when he fell. Whatever the reasons, his decision to oppose Richard was a godsend for Margaret and the Lancastrian cause.

As a result of the information from his agents in the west Richard despatched troops to capture the vital bridges and crossings over the River Severn. It was quickly done and meant that when Buckingham finally marched, he found the crossings held against him and the river, swollen after a violent storm that hit the country on 15 October, otherwise impassable.

Buckingham was clearly in an untenable position. He could not cross the Severn and could not retreat because his castles and estates back in South Wales had been seized almost as soon as he had left. Sir Thomas Vaughan of Tretower captured Brecon Castle within a few days of Buckingham leaving. He fled to Wem where he was betrayed by his servant Humphrey Bannister and captured. He was executed on 2 November 1483, in a courtyard located between the Blue Boar and Saracen's Head Inns near Salisbury.

Buckingham's fate had been sealed the moment he failed to cross the Severn. What remains unexplainable is the leniency that Richard displayed towards Margaret Beaufort. He had every reason to execute her, but she was spared. The only punishment she received was the loss of her titles and estates, but even this was a mild reproach as these were immediately passed on to her husband, Lord Stanley. It was a degree of leniency that would, in the years ahead, come back to haunt Richard III.

And what of Henry Tudor, what was he doing while the rebellion stuttered and failed? He had been amply funded and supplied by Duke Francis who, as well as large sums of money, presented him with seven ships and many soldiers. By the time his fleet set sail at the end of October it was a significant gathering of troops and ships. Henry was almost beside himself with excitement – surely the time had come to finally reclaim the throne of England for the House of Lancaster?

Unfortunately, weather once more played a hand. Severe gales in the Channel scattered Henry's fleet of fifteen warships, and only his vessel and one other managed to reach the English coast, making landfall in the Poole/Plymouth area. When dawn broke on 19 October Henry saw that he was off Poole harbour. More worryingly, the shore was lined with ranks of soldiers. Henry was expecting to meet up with the Duke of Buckingham and several people on board his ship felt that these men might be an advance party from his army:-

> But erle Henry suspecting yt to be a trick, as yt was in dede,
> after that he dyd see none of owne ships within view, hoysted
> up sale and with proserus wind came into Normandy.
> (Polydore Vergil: Anglica Historia, Books 23–25)

After waiting some time for his missing ships, Henry had finally realised they were never going to come and ventured closer to land. The soldiers along the quayside were by now shouting that they had been sent by the Duke of Buckingham and that he should come ashore to join them in finishing off a defeated Richard. Henry was no fool and quickly realised that these were not Buckingham's men, they were in fact Richard's. As Polydore Vergil said, he immediately ordered a return to Brittany. There he learned of the fate of Buckingham and the other rebels and realised quite how lucky he had been.

Henry was somewhat mollified when news reached him that the Marquess of Dorset and several other fugitives from Richard's regime had arrived in Vannes:-

> He then rightly believed that his cause, instead of being
> ruined, was now strengthened. He sent for the refugees to
> meet him in Rennes – On Christmas Day 1483 they all met in
> the Cathedral and ratified all agreements by plighting their
> troth. Henry then promised that as soon as he became King
> he would marry Elizabeth, Edward IV's eldest daughter.
> (S.B. Chrimes: *Henry VII*, p.27)

The Buckingham rebellion might have failed but Henry's plans were slowly gaining momentum. He simply did not need to be rushed.

X X X

The disaster of the Buckingham Rebellion did not deter Henry and in the summer of 1484 he assembled another fleet, again funded largely by the Duke of Brittany. But for some reason it never sailed. For the moment Henry and Jasper remained at Vannes, but their long sojourn in Brittany was now coming to an end.

In 1484 Duke Francis again fell ill. This time it was serious, his fragile physical and mental health continuing to decline, and governance of Brittany was temporarily taken over by the duke's treasurer Pierre Landais. With an eye to sensible finance, Landais saw that the duke had been expending large sums of money in his support of the two Tudor earls. Apart from whatever else Henry had been given, funding and providing two fleets would not have been a minor investment.

There were over 400 English exiles in the town of Vannes alone, a somewhat riotous crew that was causing considerable strain on the local economy. In the mind of the duke's treasurer something had to be done, and it had to be done before Francis recovered.

Landais was also acutely conscious of the threat posed by Brittany's neighbour France. The French king Louis XI had died in 1483, being succeeded by Charles VIII who was still a minor. In light of his young age, control of the country was a debatable matter, both the Duke of Orleans and Anne of Beaujeu, the sister of the new king, vying for power. The in-fighting in the French court gave him time and Landais came to an agreement with Richard that, in exchange for military and financial aid against France, he would return Henry to England.

Henry and Jasper were warned by John Morton, Bishop of Flanders, another refugee from Richard's kingdom, of the proposal. They immediately knew that their time in Brittany was at an end and secretly asked permission from the French royal family to move to France. Anne eagerly agreed – possession of the two Tudors would be a great bargaining tool to use against the Duke of Orleans.

Their escape from Brittany was cleverly done. First Jasper left Vannes, supposedly to visit the sick Francis who was recuperating at Rennes near the French border. At the last moment he and his party veered off and crossed the border into France. Two days later Henry followed him. He took with him a change of clothes and, dressed as a serving man, he rode hard for Anjou where he soon rejoined his uncle. For the time being at least they were safe.

It had been a close call. Henry had not asked permission to leave Brittany, the country that had protected him all these years, and when it became clear that he had gone he was immediately pursued. He reached Anjou just one hour ahead of the chasing riders.

In the early months of 1485 Richard had flirted with the idea that he might marry Elizabeth of York, the daughter of his dead brother. Richard's wife, Anne Neville, had died in March that year – indeed, there were rumours circulating that he had poisoned her in order to be able to marry his niece – and as his popularity declined those rumours only increased. Such a marriage would at least prevent Elizabeth from marrying Henry, but the rumours and the opposition were so strong that Richard was forced to make a declaration at the Guildhall that he had no intention of taking Elizabeth as a wife.

Henry noted Richard's discomfiture with pleasure. The idea of Richard marrying Elizabeth had worried him. Any union between Richard and the Woodville family could spell only disaster for Henry who needed as much support as he could gather for his proposed invasion. He had already pledged to marry Elizabeth himself and unite the two warring royal houses, but if Richard had got there ahead of him it would have foiled his carefully laid plans. The affair convinced him that he could not delay much longer. Soon he would have to take the great gamble, leave France and return to England.

Richard's unpopularity continued to grow. A short poem by William Collingbourne, written in 1484, just prior to Henry's invasion, summed up the attitude of many in the country:-

> The Cat, the Rat and Lovell our Dog
> Rule all England under a Hog.
>
> (Collingbourne, quoted in Carradice p.38,
> Skidmore p.174 et al)

Cat in the poem refers to Richard's friend and advisor William Catesby, next to Richard one of the most despised men in England. Rat was Richard Ratcliffe, Lovell the Dog was Lord Lovell and the Hog was an obvious reference to Richard and his emblem of a boar.

The poem had been nailed to the door of St Paul's Cathedral on 18 July and was eagerly read by early morning worshippers. The poem was torn down and the author arrested. Collingbourne was tried for treason, found guilty and hanged, drawn and quartered – a terrible end for a piece of pure doggerel that did manage to touch the heart of the problem in Richard's England.

In England there had always been antipathy between the people of the north and those from the south. The king's support in the north was well grounded but, increasingly, the noblemen from the south began turning against him. Many of them slipped quietly out of the country and joined Henry Tudor, first in Brittany and then in France.

One of those who hastened away to join Henry in Paris was John de Vere, the Earl of Oxford. A veteran of battles like Barnet, Oxford was a formidable warrior and he was accompanied by two redoubtable fighting men, James Blunt and John Fortescue. All three of them were a welcome addition to Henry's forces:-

> Whan Henry saw the erle he was ravisshyd with joy incredible
> that a man of so great nabilytie and knowledge in the warres,
> and most perfyte and sound fytelytie, most earnestly bent to
> his syde.
>
> (Polydore Vergil, Books 23-25)

Henry was sure that he had a firm cohort of friends and allies in England and Wales. Thomas and William Stanley had both sent him letters of support, as had Gilbert Talbot. Secret messages confirmed that, in Wales, Rhys ap Thomas and John Savage were both willing to pledge their allegiance to him. It boded well for a return to Britain.

Duke Francis of Brittany might have been excused for feeling let down by the sudden departure of Henry but as he slowly recovered his strength he saw that, in reality, the young man had had no choice. England was the last place he needed to be right now. Francis was determined to undo at least some of the damage that Landais had caused.

Henry and Jasper had left almost 500 supporters behind them in Brittany. These men Francis could have easily sent back to England where they would have faced certain death. He chose the other way and allowed the rebels to join Henry in Paris. He even gave them money, about 700 livres, to pay for their travel. Henry was touched by the kindness of the duke and never forgot the debt he owed him.

Jasper had always sensed the viability of Wales as a base for an invasion. He knew the country well and was regarded as something of a hero by the populace. He knew the feelings of the ordinary Welsh people as well as the noblemen and landed gentry. They had no love for England or for Richard. Henry, having been born in Pembroke, was one of them, not one of the hated 'Sais' (English). With Henry now the senior Lancastrian claimant to the throne, Jasper laid the ground well – Henry was coming as a Welsh prince, he let people know, someone who would redress all of the wrongs incurred by a humiliated and humbled people over hundreds of years.

In his book *Henry VII*, S.B. Chrimes states that the Welsh connections and ancestry of Henry tend to be over exaggerated:-

> His father Edmund – was by descent French and Welsh; his mother, Margaret Beaufort, was English; his grandfather Owen Tudor was indeed wholly Welsh but his grandmother Catherine of Valois was partly French and partly Bavarian.
>
> (Chrimes, p.3)

That may be so, but playing on Henry's Welsh ancestry was deliberately and cleverly done. Jasper certainly made great political capital out of Henry's Welsh connections. The Tudors came from an old Anglesey family, one that claimed descent from Cadwaladr, the legendary ancient British king, and Jasper made sure that the red dragon of the old monarch was prominently displayed on Henry's banners and regalia. Henry was, he declared, Y Mab Darogan, the Son of Prophesy.

Jasper actively encouraged the Welsh bards to run a propaganda mission on behalf of Henry. They needed little encouragement, having long claimed prophetic vision and written about someone coming to deliver the country from the oppression of the Saxons – in other words the English.

Owain Glyndŵr, the great Welsh rebel and leader, had disappeared when his rebellion ran out of steam at the beginning of the century. Legend, fuelled by the bards, said that he was merely sleeping in a cave in the mountains and would soon return to free the Welsh of the tyranny they had suffered for years. What was Henry if he was not a reincarnation of Glyndŵr:-

> Now their expectations were concentrated on the exiled Prince – No less than thirty five bards wrote these 'vaticinatory' poems.
>
> (David Williams: *Modern Wales* pp.18/19)

Welsh bardic poetry was largely an oral skill with very little ever written down. The poems were passed from one person to another and when the bard died his poems invariably died with him. The poems about the coming of a

39

liberator kept the Welsh people in a 'ferment of expectation' but it has meant that few, if any, of the prophesy poems of the time now exist. (Williams, p.19)

The threat was implicit and it was strong. More importantly, it was a message, one that everyone in England and Wales could understand only too well. Henry Tudor was coming.

Richard was well aware that another invasion attempt was imminent and began to prepare himself and his country to repel it. He began with clamping down on the freedom of Margaret Beaufort, forcing her husband Lord Stanley to dismiss her servants and keep her close by his side at all times.

Richard knew that Henry's mother had been behind Buckingham's recent rebellion and the attempted invasion. She might now, with Henry clearly preparing to coma again, have expected harsher treatment but, as Vergil later wrote 'the working of a woman's wit was thowght of smaule accounte.' (Polydore Vergil, Books 23–25)

Richard then turned to propaganda and to a charm offensive. He issued a proclamation promising clemency and forgiveness for anyone who had gone over to Henry's side. It met with some success. Several high ranking noblemen returned to the fold, something that pleased the king but disturbed Henry. Was his cause beginning to lose power and direction, he asked himself?

When Thomas, Marquess of Dorset, defected from Paris, Henry was even more worried. The Marquess was a significant public figure, someone who would provide Richard with exactly the sort of propaganda coup he desired. He also had knowledge of all Henry's plans. If he should return to England and throw himself on Richard's mercy, everything would be lost.

Henry knew he had to act quickly. With the agreement of King Charles he had the man hunted down and brought back to him. Dorset's flight had been a bitter blow for Henry and for Jasper Tudor:-

> The marquess's escape had revealed the divisions in his own camp over which he was struggling to control and maintain discipline.
>
> (Skidmore: *Bosworth, the Birth of the Tudors* p.197)

Henry knew that he could never trust Dorset again, one of the reasons he later left the man in France, as surety for money borrowed from the French to launch his invasion.

Meanwhile Richard's preparations began to take on a more military air. New armaments were ordered, including gunpowder, lead and a number of new serpentines (cannons). Commissions of Array – instructions to local gentry and office holders – were issued with a view to raising troops in the name of the king.

All of that, of course, cost money and the king immediately demanded loans from the nobles and gentry. Money was also requested from the church. Richard had been confidently assured that a sum in the region of £10,000 would soon materialise but the response was lack lustre; less than half the expected amount came in.

Francis, Lord Lovell was ordered to prepare a fleet and keep watch on the coast around Southampton while Richard himself moved his court to Nottingham. It was more central than London and would enable him to march swiftly to whichever part of the country was under threat from the Tudors. He also ordered the Great Seal, normally kept in London, to be brought to him at Nottingham so that all orders and commissions would bear the authority of the king.

There was an assumption that the yeomen and ordinary men who would make up the bulk of his army would be expert in archery and fighting. However, there had been no significant battle in the country since Tewkesbury in 1471 and the campaigns in France, expeditions that had led to the English archers being considered the finest in the world, had long been over.

The men of England, therefore, had little recent experience of warfare. It would be wrong to say that they were living off the reputations of their forefathers – the vast majority neither knew nor cared what people thought of their military prowess. They had no desire to join anybody's army and fight in battle. Many of those who would, in times of crisis, become foot soldiers in Richard's army owned neither the weapons nor the armour to help them fulfil their tasks. They were, effectively, amateurs.

This was in complete contrast to Henry's supporters and soldiers in France. By now he was being treated by Charles as the true King of England and in May the French monarch informed his advisors and the Estates (the French Parliament) that he was prepared to fund with money and with soldiers 'his dearly beloved cousin'.

Apart from having strong Lancastrian family connections, Charles was decidedly hostile to Richard. It was an emotion dating back to the invasion of France led by Richard and his brother King Edward in 1475.

Richard had been opposed to the Treaty of Picquigny which had ended the campaign before it had really begun and effectively bought off King Edward and his troops. He had been so angry that he refused to be present for the signing of the treaty. It was a position and attitude that Charles would neither forget nor forgive.

The thought of another Richard-backed invasion of his country was always present at the forefront of the French king's mind. There was also the memory of the Hundred Years War, a devastating century of carnage that was far too recent to allow any French monarch to sleep easily at night. At least with Henry there were family connections to help keep the peace.

Anything that would hinder Richard was good policy and if, by some chance, he should be removed from the throne, well, that would be so much better still.

Charles now agreed to loan Henry 40,000 livres tournois towards the cost of his invasion, the money to be doled out in instalments. It is unlikely that Henry ever received more than the first payment of 10,000 livres but it was at least something.

Henry had some capital given to him by his mother for the express purpose of launching an invasion but he needed more, much more. Paying for soldiers, as well as equipping and feeding them, was an expensive business. Not everyone was driven by the dreams of Henry and Jasper and if there were not enough volunteers, then troops would have to be bought.

As a result Henry was forced to borrow 30,000 livres, a personal loan, from Phillippe Lullier, one of Charles's advisors and councillors. He had nothing to offer as surety, apart from his personal possessions and men. His possessions meant very little – in a few weeks he would either be King of England, which would make him inordinately rich, or dead. Either way he had no need of them.

The issue of men was equally as immaterial to him. He was not entirely unhappy to leave behind the Marquess of Dorset and John Bourgchier, the 19-year-old Lord FitzWarin. Dorset had already proved his unreliability and FitzWarin was still an untried teenager. The two men were handed over as a guarantee against the loan and as hostages.

By the summer of 1485 Henry was ready. He felt he had already delayed too long and every day he waited, Richard grew stronger and more powerful. He might have considered landing in Cornwall or Devon but the Marquess of Dorset and Lord FitzWarin who had most influence in the West Country had been left behind as surety. Instead he would follow Jasper's advice and aim for Wales.

His spies had already told him that West Wales was not well defended, Richard having left defence of the region to noblemen like Rhys ap Thomas and Sir William Herbert. He had even withdrawn several of the ships that were supposed to protect the Welsh coast. For someone as suspicious and aware of treachery as Richard it seems to have been a rather foolish oversight and one that would undoubtedly come back to haunt him.

It was imperative that Henry got ashore before Richard could send more troops to the area. It was something that worried Jasper, Oxford and Henry as they prepared to sail. And that was not all. The possibility of the English king taking Elizabeth of York as a bride was also still there, nagging away at Henry's memory. Richard might well have stated he had no intention of marrying his niece, but Henry's paranoia would not allow him to trust Richard.

The exact number of troops under Henry's command is a little unclear, some reports stating that he had very few soldiers, perhaps as few as 1,000, others estimating the total at 4,500.

Polydor Vergil puts the figure at a mere 2,000 and that was a figure he must have got from Henry himself. Henry, like Vergil however, would have been more than likely to provide information that put him in the best possible light and there was no way he was ever likely to reveal the exact number of troops at his disposal. He had defeated Richard despite all the odds, and that included inferior numbers in his army:-

> He lowsyd from the mouth of the Seyne with two thousand onely of armyd men and a few shippes – he came unto Wales the 7th day after, a little before soone set.
>
> (Polydore Vergil, Books 23–25)

The true figure is probably somewhere between Vergil's 2,000 and the larger total, more than likely somewhere in the region of 3,000 men. Quantity was one thing, quality was something else and it is certain that Henry's army was, at best, rather a mixed crew.

As well as his 500 rebel companions from England there were also 1,000 Scots under the immediate command of Sir Alexander Bruce and

Sir Bernard Stewart. These troops were serving the King of France at the time, mercenaries who had sold their skills and abilities as soldiers, and came as a gift from Charles.

Henry also had the services of around 2,000 French mercenaries. These had been provided by Philippe de Crevecouer, Marshal of France, but they were at best a somewhat disreputable and truculent group whose behaviour was both troublesome and dangerous.

Crevecouer chose to remain in the background, not joining the invasion force himself but delegating command of the French troops to the young Philibert de Chandee. It would certainly not have helped his plans if he was found to be accompanying his mercenaries.

At first sight these French soldiers were just what Henry and Jasper needed. They would, it was felt, instil fear into Richard and his supporters and show no mercy when it came to combat. Hardened brawlers, they were not the type of men to make your friends, but then Henry was not intending to make friends with Richard. He wanted to kill him.

The French mercenaries brought more than military experience to Britain with Henry. They also brought the infamous sweating sickness. An affliction similar to the influenza epidemic that hit Europe in the days after 1918, it was a virulent illness – all too often you were well in the morning, as someone once said, and dead by evening. The cause was unknown, the cure equally as mysterious and nobody knew how to avoid it if it hit your locality:-

> This disease was certainly known in England previously, as
> Thomas Stanley told Richard that he was suffering from it,
> as an excuse for not joining him a few days before Bosworth.
> (Chrimes, p.40)

Known or not, the sweating sickness of the French soldiers did not help Henry in the organisation of his march or when formulating his battle plans. It was yet another problem he had to deal with, part of the worries and concerns of any commander in chief.

With Frenchmen and French-serving Scotsmen having been placed at his service it meant that Henry's invading army was made up principally of foreigners. On consideration, that was hardly the most reassuring of facts as invading foreign armies were not thought well of anywhere, but were particularly reviled in England and Wales.

As an island nation the country's protecting seas had given the people a subconscious but profound sense of independence. Anything, however small or large, that threated that self-contained idea of uniqueness was immediately disliked, even hated.

Memories were long and the Norman Conquest of 1066 was not that distant an event. Closer still, only eighty years before, in 1400, Owain Glyndŵr had landed in Milford Haven with an army of French mercenaries. Regardless of whom they supported, Glyndŵr's rebellion and subsequent invasion had brought discord and confusion to the Welsh and English countryside.

Jasper had told Henry many times that the Welsh would flock to his banner as soon as he landed. Henry hoped his uncle was accurate in his judgement as the French mercenaries provided by Crevecouer might have been numerous but, as he soon found out, they were far from reliable.

He had been happy to accept them as part of his army, but on closer inspection the mercenaries had proved to be not all skilled and many of them did not even have weapons with which to fight a pitched battle.

Their behaviour was increasingly delinquent as they waited to take ship to England, but Henry was hardly in a position to reject Crevecoeur's offer of troops. He might need whatever soldiers he could get, but more than anything Henry needed the Welsh to come flocking to his side.

Crevecouer had not been entirely altruistic in his gift and the band of mercenary soldiers had been carefully chosen. He was a politician and wheeler-dealer of some note and, far from helping Henry in his attempt on the English throne, Crevecouer had an altogether more selfish motive in mind.

Regardless of who won the coming confrontation, if these mercenaries could sow discord in English ranks it might distract the attention of the English crown and enable him to snatch back the port and town of Calais. His aim was to foment nothing less than more civil war in England, a return to the worst days of the Wars of the Roses.

The town of Calais in northern France was now the only part of France still under English control and Crevecouer and other French statesmen were desperate to see it returned to its rightful ownership. It was a distant, somewhat ethereal hope, but Crevecouer clung to his dream and duly organised Henry's mercenary army.

Henry could not have cared less about the Marshal's motives. He had his soldiers and he had his ships. He was sure that his time had finally come.

Chapter Five

The Return

Henry Tudor left Harfleur on the River Seine on 1 August 1485. The wind was in his favour, a gentle breeze that propelled his ships easily and sedately towards England. Henry's fleet of thirty vessels carried his soldiers, all of their equipment, their horses and enough provisions to get them through the six or seven day journey.

Richard had guessed wrongly. Their destination was not England but Milford Haven in Wales which meant that Lord Lovell was doing nothing more than wasting his time patrolling the sea lanes outside Southampton.

Henry's fleet might have been heading for Milford but an exact landing site had not yet been identified. The Haven was a wide and glorious expanse of sheltered water with plenty of places where an invading army could come ashore. Wherever they chose it would be close enough to the area of South Pembrokeshire that both Henry and his Uncle Jasper knew well.

The expedition was, in many respects, a case of 'last chance saloon' for Henry. Far from being the last throw of the dice by a desperate man, Richard's recent appeals and offers to those who had fled his court in order to join Henry had unnerved the Earl of Richmond. He knew how fickle men could be and he had watched with growing concern as the less convinced of his followers drifted back to the service of the king. For Henry and the whole Tudor cause it was certainly now or never.

On the other hand, although Henry did not yet know it, Richard's preparations had not gone well either. He had not been sent the money he expected, nor the troops. He was having to chase up promised but undelivered bands of soldiers and in the case of cities like York, which had totally ignored his Commission of Array, remind them of their obligations.

The lack of response from York was just one worrying matter for Richard. The fact that the city was in the control of the Earl of

Northumberland, one of the traditionally rebellious Percy family, was only made worse by the knowledge that Northumberland and Henry had been friends and companions during their time at Raglan Castle under the wardship of Lord Herbert. Where did Northumberland's loyalty really lie, Richard repeatedly asked himself? For the king, as for Henry Tudor, it was now a matter of do or die.

The king's court was alive with rumours about Henry's coming. Everyone appeared to have an opinion or some new and fascinating piece of information that changed and developed by the day. There was even talk about Henry intending to land at Milford – but which Milford did they mean, the one in Wales or the port on the south coast?

After consideration Richard had thought that, if the rumour was correct, it would probably be the south coast; one of the reasons he had ordered Lord Lovell to patrol with the fleet off Southampton. With luck, he thought, Lovell would destroy Henry's ships long before they reached shore.

With all of the strategic skill of an experienced general, Richard's own position at Nottingham had been carefully chosen. He could make a forced march in whichever direction he chose, depending on where Henry finally landed. His problem was not location, however. It remained a lack of good quality fighting men.

Welsh poets or bards were now writing openly about Henry's coming, stressing the fact that he was arriving to deliver the Welsh from the oppression of the English. The following poem, while its exact date of origin remains unknown, makes a clear reference to Richard in the character of 'the Boar.' Part verse, part prophesy, part wishful thinking, the poem has to originate from the reign of King Richard:-

> Full well I wend
> That in the end
> Richmond sprung from British race
> From out this land the Boar shall chase.
> (Unknown author, fifteenth-century poem)

The white boar was Richard's personal insignia, just as Henry's was the Welsh dragon. How much of this creative flowering Richard knew remains a matter of speculation, but with his extensive spy network it is unlikely that he was not fully aware of the mood in the country.

Henry's mind was eased somewhat when, just before he sailed, a messenger by the name of John Morgan arrived with news from his mother. In her letter Margaret Beaufort stated that Rhys ap Thomas, the most powerful man in West Wales, the person to whom Richard had entrusted the safety of the region, was willing to give him support. It was exactly the sort of news he needed. In fact Rhys was far less sure about changing his allegiance from Richard to Henry than anyone knew, but at that stage of the adventure Henry was prepared to take the news at face value.

It was, therefore, in a mood of trepidation and excitement that Henry Tudor finally set sail. So much was, as yet, unclear. His army was hardly the most efficient of units and the degree of support that he could expect from his countrymen remained an unknown factor. His invasion was a gamble but it was one on which he was prepared to risk his life.

X X X

The voyage was uneventful, fine weather for once aiding Henry. Rather than the gale that had scattered his ships and hindered his previous attempt at invasion, now he had balmy breezes and a fine calm sea. The fleet made good progress and after several days at sea the looming landmass of the British Isles began to take shape on the horizon. There are no records to show Henry's feelings at this time but he must have been consumed by self-belief tinged with a lingering shred of apprehension. He had prepared as well as he could; now it was time for action.

Arriving at the mouth of Milford Haven in the late afternoon or early evening of 7 August – just before sunset as Vergil wrote – Henry could not wait to get ashore. But now, once again, legend and fact become mixed. Popular opinion states that he landed at Mill Bay, a tiny beach just inside the Haven mouth. There is even a plaque on the cliff above the beach to commemorate the event. But the question has to be asked – is this accurate?

According to legend Henry came ashore at the eastern end of Mill Bay, at a spot once known as Harri's Carthorse but now covered by rock fall. The story has him kneeling on the sand and kissing it before reciting Psalm 43 – 'Judge me, O Lord, and favour my cause.' He then knighted eight of his most significant followers, effectively binding them to him and to his crusade. Included in the list of newly knighted men were Edward Courtenay and the French commander Philibert de Chandee.

The French contingent, however, was seemingly reluctant to land and had to be bribed or cajoled with fresh food and drink. Once the army was disembarked, they headed inland, away from Mill Bay towards the village and castle of Dale which lay some two miles distant. There was only one path off the beach, a steep uphill climb along a narrow track that followed the course of a small stream. It was muddy and thick with clumps of coarse grass and bushes which caused Henry to remark, 'Brunt going, men, brunt going.' By brunt going he meant hard going and Brunt Farm, just inland from the beach, was supposedly named after Henry's words. That, at least, is the legend.

As a landing beach for an invasion Mill Bay was then, and remains now, a singularly inappropriate site. To begin with it is small, barely a hundred yards in width. Landing two or three boatloads of soldiers at any one time would have been the most that could be hoped for. With thirty vessels anchored off shore and all trying to unload men and supplies there would have been an enormous log jam at the beach head. There would inevitably have been accidents, boats upset and possibly even men drowned. There appears to be no record of any such happenings.

Given those factors, the idea of putting 3,000 men ashore on this isolated and rather inaccessible strip of sand and shingle remains a fairly ludicrous option. Arguably it could have been done but it would have taken many hours of hard, back-breaking work. And time was something that Henry did not have.

At low tide the water level in Milford Haven drops remarkably and at Mill Bay low water displays dozens of jagged rock pillars that would, even when the tide was full, have made short work of wooden sailing ships. None of them would have been able to come closer than a hundred yards from the beach. There was no jetty and so the landing would have had to be done by long boats from each individual ship in the fleet, a time-consuming business that would have been accompanied by shouts, calls and the scream of frightened horses.

It was already getting on for dusk when Henry's forces began to disembark. Even disregarding the time needed to persuade the reluctant French mercenaries to go ashore there is no way that the whole army could have reached the beach before darkness finally fell. It would not have been physically possible.

With just one way off the beach – the narrow, slippery track – it would also have been a huge tactical error to choose Mill Bay. Any defending forces would have had to do little more than sit at the top of the incline and pour fire down onto the advancing men. The narrowness of the pathway would not have allowed any invading army to deploy in line abreast. Moving up the track would have had to be done virtually in single file and would have given them, at best, a front of no more than two men – tactical suicide.

One argument used to support the choice of Mill Bay is the fact that Henry and Jasper wanted to keep the landing secret. If that was in any way true it was a forlorn hope before the exercise even began. The fleet consisted of approximately thirty ships, no mean collection of vessels, no matter how big or small they might have been.

The nearest enemy outpost was Dale Castle, barely 2 miles away and while Henry had no idea of how many men were garrisoned there, they would have been aware of his arrival the moment the fleet entered the Haven beneath St Ann's Head. By the time his ships dropped anchor everyone in the immediate locality would have known of their presence. Mill Bay might well be hidden from Dale Castle but a fleet of thirty ships would have stretched around the headland and out into the waterway, thus becoming immediately visible to anyone in the fortress.

A warning light or beacon was situated in an old disused chapel high up on St Ann's Head, the first of many lights that would be lit once Henry's invading fleet was sighted. This beacon was part of a chain and was supplemented by others further along the waterway. These were the means by which news of his coming was flashed to Pembroke Castle 7 or 8 miles upriver. As soon as he received the message Richard Williams, the constable of the castle, immediately took horse for Nottingham. The journey of 210 miles took him four days and nights of solid riding, meaning that Richard had been made aware of the landing by II August.

If the constable of Pembroke Castle could hear of Henry's landing within a few hours of it taking place, the men in Dale Castle would have known about it far sooner. The idea of a 'quiet landing' promptly goes out of the window. Apart from anything else, the noise of disembarking men would have been another warning for waiting defenders. It would have been impossible to land in silence, thus destroying the rationale of choosing Mill Bay in the first place.

A recently erected statue of Henry Tudor, in the shadow of Pembroke Castle.

Above left: King Henry VI.

Above right: Margaret of Anjou.

Above left: Jasper and Edmund Tudor.

Above right: The Battle of Tewkesbury, one of the bloodiest engagements of the Wars of the Roses.

The bloody and decisive Battle of Towton.

The mighty
fortress of
Pembroke,
birthplace of
a king.

Suscinio Castle
where Henry
spent many of
his exile years.

The young Margaret Beaufort, mother of
Henry Tudor.

The famous portrait of the Princes in the Tower.

Above left: The young Henry Tudor.

Above right: Richard of Gloucester, King Richard III.

Mill Bay, the supposed
landing site of Henry
and his troops.

Another view of tiny,
rocky Mill Bay.

Lord Thomas Stanley, Henry's potential ally.

The field of Battle.

Richard awakens after his nightmare, David Garrick playing the role of Richard in Shakespeare's play.

Plate armour of the style worn by well-off knights and soldiers at the time of Bosworth Field.

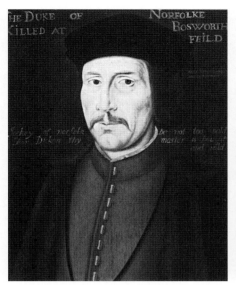

Above left: John Howard, Duke of Norfolk.

Above right: Henry receives the crown, a romantic but inaccurate image.

King Richard in the heat of the battle. He would probably have used a battle hammer rather than a sword.

The Battle of Bosworth Field.

Above left: King Henry in later days.

Above right: Perkin Warbeck, pretender and claimant of Henry's throne.

Henry VII on his deathbed.

Interestingly, Polydore Vergil – who was writing relatively close to the event – does not mention either Mill Bay or any other landing site. He contents himself with a simple throwaway line about what Henry did first:-

He (Henry) took first a place the name whereof ys Dalley.
(Polydor Vergil, Books 23–25)

For 'Dalley' read Dale! The modern acceptance of Mill Bay as the landing site seems to derive from an article written by S.B. Chrimes of Cardiff University in the 'Welsh History Review' of 1965. He acknowledges that little hard evidence is available but then makes a judgement that is based as much on personal preference as it is upon hard fact. Most historians and writers have since taken his words at face value and Mill Bay has become the accepted location for the landing.

The article itself is interesting but it is as much a viewpoint as it is an informed opinion. Chrimes begins by dismissing the view of Elizabethan writer George Owen, who stated that the landing took place at Dale. According to Owen, Henry later built a chapel at Dale to commemorate the event but no such chapel has been found. If it ever existed it has been long demolished and this seems to be the main reason for Chrimes disregarding Owen's words.

Chrimes links the landing site to Henry's well-recorded statement – 'Brunt going, men.' The word 'brunt' does not seem to derive from Pembrokeshire dialect, as many have believed. Chrimes quotes Pembrokeshire historian Edward Laws in believing that the farm which bears the name was already in existence when Henry came ashore. Henry, he says, was making a pun that joined the hard going of the climb to the brunt or crux of a battle and using the name of the farm to hammer home his point – all of which is feasible.

He then narrows down the choice to just two places, despite the fact that the Haven has no fewer than sixteen creeks and five bays, all of which could possibly have functioned as a landing site. The two locations he comes down to are Angle on the other side of the Haven and Mill Bay.

King Richard himself had already offered Angle as the site of the landing. In a letter to Henry Vernon, a squire of his court, written on II August, just after he received news that Henry had finally arrived, the king declared that Henry Tudor and his troops had come ashore at Angle, or Nangle as the village and bay were then known :-

> Our rebelles and traitours departed out of the water of the Seine the first day of this present month, making their cours westwards ben landed at Nangle besides Mylford Haven in Wales on Sunday last.
>
> (Appendix Part IV, of the 12th Report of the Historical MSS Commission, p.7)

If, as Henry believed on that August evening, Rhys ap Thomas was prepared to support him in his enterprise, Richard's guess at Angle would be a logical choice. It was a fine, sheltered anchorage and Carew Castle, the favourite of all Rhys's many houses and castles, was just a few miles beyond Pembroke. It could be reached within a few hours. The little matter of Pembroke Castle was something that needed to be dealt with but if, as with so many of the fortresses in West Wales, it was lightly fortified and equipped, it would not be an insurmountable problem.

At the end of the day, however, Chrimes comes down in favour of Mill Bay, basing his choice on three factors. One: Mill Bay was the first available beach after St Ann's Head. Two: it was identified as the site by H. Thornhill Timmins in his book *Nooks and Corners of Pembrokeshire* published in 1895. Three: historian Edward Laws states that Henry came ashore at a place called Brunt.

No one can deny his first point; Mill Bay is certainly the first bay and beach inside the Haven. If Henry was eager to get ashore this would be a possible choice. It would not have been perfect – from the sea it looks to be little more than a tiny rocky cove – but it would have been available.

Without wishing to demean Thornhill Timmins, his book is exactly as the title suggests a slight-telling of local tales that does not have any pretence to scholarly research and writing. It is basically a book for the fireside or for tourists and cannot be regarded as a work of great academic importance. It is certainly not a work on which you should base a theory or serious scholarly proposal.

Lastly, Edward Laws does not mention Mill Bay in any of his writings. Brunt Farm, which he does write about, is an isolated farm house, not a village. It is situated as close to Dale as it is to the bay in question and at no stage does he say that for Brunt you should read Mill Bay.

The fact needs reiterating. Brunt, as described or mentioned by Laws, clearly does not have to mean Mill Bay. It could quite as easily have been Dale, a fact that Chrimes conveniently ignores. He makes the claim for Mill Bay again in his later book on Henry, this time adding that W. Dane Russell had made a similar claim in 1916. (Chrimes, p.40) On such flimsy evidence the whole case for Mill Bay being the landing site is based.

Geologist and author Roger MacCallum has sailed into and past Mill Bay on many occasions. He remains clear that Mill Bay would have been a totally unsuitable location for any sort of landing in those days of wooden warships and galleons:-

> Mill Bay is a rock encircled, boulder strewn bay just inside the entrance to Milford Haven on the western side. Although sheltered from westerly and south-westerly winds, being tucked behind St Ann's Head, it is commonly subject to Atlantic swells which refract around St Ann's Head and surge into the bay. An area of sand is exposed in the bay for a few hours over low tide; the top of the beach narrows between rocks, becoming funnel shaped, and is comprised of stones and boulders leading to a rough path to the cliff top.
>
> Submerged offshore, particularly in the northern half of the bay, are patches of rock and boulders reaching as much as 20ft above the surrounding seabed. The topography of the bay would seem to make it an ill-advised place to anchor ships or to carry out an amphibious landing, particularly when just a short distance away is the whole of Milford Haven estuary with its numerous safe anchorages, bays and beaches where a landing would have been much safer and easier.
>
> (MacCallum: Letter to the Author, 2018)

MacCallum is convinced that there is little, if any, contemporary evidence that Mill Bay was where the landing took place. Most of the opinions expressed by writers, he says, seem to rest more in local tradition, legend and folklore than they ever do on factual evidence.

His own choice for the landing site is interesting:-

> The plaque at the cliff top above the bay tells us that Henry landed in Mill Bay but that the invasion fleet sailed on and

landed at Dale, a short distance to the north. Dale Bay had been renowned as a safe anchorage for centuries and has good landing on hard sand with more than enough room for Henry's fleet. That Henry's fleet came ashore here is recounted by the noted Pembrokeshire antiquarian George Owen of Henllys.

(MacCallum, 2018)

Here MacCallum might have hit on the truth of what really happened. Seeing his homeland – and, in particular, the county of his birth – for the first time in fourteen years it is entirely feasible that he wanted to go ashore at the first opportunity. It would have been partly from sheer delight in seeing Pembrokeshire again and partly from a desire to say a prayer of thanksgiving for his return.

If this was indeed the case, Henry and a small party of supporters and bodyguards could well have come ashore at Mill Bay. From there he could despatch scouts to find out how well defended Dale Castle really was and, when they returned with the news that the fortress was lightly garrisoned, order the fleet to sail on to Dale Bay.

The anchorage at Dale was safe and sheltered. Here Henry could have used the tide to his favour. Rather than disembark the troops by longboat, the ships could have simply pulled onto the sand and, when the tide fell, allow the men to be discharged directly onto the beach. When the tide flooded the ships would be refloated. It is supposition, but it is logical.

The other possibility is that soldiers could have been disembarked by boat, in the normal fashion. The sand at Dale is certainly wide and sheltered enough to allow many longboats to come ashore at the same time.

The other option for the landing, which S.B. Chrimes eventually dismisses, is Angle. King Richard might have believed this to be the landing site but there are no traditions or legends to say that this is where Henry came ashore. It remains an option only if Rhys ap Thomas was at Carew Castle at the time. In fact he was then in Carmarthen.

If any type of landing had occurred at Angle it would have been by only a small detachment of men, sent to establish the military strength of Pembroke and Carew Castles. If men were put ashore here they would have later crossed the River Cleddau and rejoined Henry's main force on its march.

Despite what was later written in the seventeenth-century *Life of Sir Rhys ap Thomas* (as he became after the Battle of Bosworth Field), Rhys did not come to Dale or Mill Bay to welcome Henry ashore and

Henry did not go to Carew to meet the Welsh nobleman. In fact the two men did not meet until several days later when they came together outside Welshpool. Early in the morning of 8 August, the day after his landing, Henry was in Haverfordwest and could not have crossed the Cleddau from Carew Castle and made the 10-mile march in time.

As for the landing site, Roger MacCallum is clear that Angle and Dale are possibilities but that Mill Bay is certainly not:-

> With the dearth of contemporary accounts and evidence, it seems unlikely that that the story and details of Henry's landing will ever be known with certainty. That an amphibious landing from 30 ships was carried out at this rocky cove (Mill Bay) seems highly unlikely since Henry was a 'local boy' and would have been aware of the many safe anchorages and landing sites in Milford Haven.
>
> So it seems much more likely that the fleet landed in the sheltered anchorage of Dale, as suggested by George Owen, or at Angle as reported in a contemporary message from Richard III.
>
> (MacCallum; 2018)

As MacCallum says it is more than probable that the exact site will never be known. Speculation and informed judgement are the best we can manage.

X X X

Regardless of where he came ashore Henry Tudor, Earl of Richmond and claimant to the throne of England, spent his first night back in Wales at the castle in Dale. There is no record of any fighting over the capture of Dale Castle and it is therefore supposed that the fortress – garrisoned by perhaps a dozen men – surrendered quickly and without fuss.

Even now, in hindsight, separating fact from fiction is a problem that continues to dog Henry's footsteps. Local legend states that he was met at Dale by Rhys ap Thomas who joined up with Henry at Mullock Bridge, two miles north of Dale:-

> Here he stood under the bridge while Henry passed over, thus absolving Rhys of his sworn allegiance to Richard III.

This legend, however, is fanciful and there is no contemporary evidence to say that it took place. Edward Laws suggests that Rhys lay prone on the shore while Henry stepped over him to achieve the same end. Laws also tells us that a banquet was held at Carew Castle where Rhys and Henry planned their strategy for the coming campaign.

(MacCallum, 2018)

The later Life of Sir Rhys further develops this story about Mullock Bridge and this is repeated by Laws (Edward Laws: *The History of Little England Beyond Wales* p.222). After describing Rhys prostrating himself below the bridge the writer adds that Henry lifted the Welshman to his feet saying that he hoped never to see Rhys brought so low again.

It is all wonderful story telling but it is about as real as Cinderella or Sleeping Beauty. When Henry landed, Rhys ap Thomas was certainly not at Carew and, contrary to what he had been originally told, Henry was disconcerted to hear that the Welshman had not yet decided to join his enterprise. There was certainly no great banquet at Carew Castle; all fantasy. What was real was the need to move – and move quickly.

Guillaume de Casenove, commander of the fleet, had already made his move. As soon as the army was ashore he hauled up his anchors and disappeared out of the Haven. Being caught against the shore by a superior fleet was a fate that no sailor wanted to endure and de Casenove, a good and careful commander, was conscious of the potential problem.

Many of the invaders, the reluctant French mercenaries in particular, must have watched the ships leave with mixed emotions. As long as the fleet was there, just off shore, there was always a way out. They were now alone in a foreign country and their fate was anything but clear.

As soon as Dale Castle was safely in his hands, Henry ordered Jasper and the Earl of Oxford to draw up the troops on open land beside the fortress so that he could address his warriors.

The moment is captured in 'The Ballad of Bosworth Field', a contemporary poem possibly written by a member of Lord Stanley's force and not, therefore, by someone present at Dale. While the main focus of the poem is on the battle, the writer does allow himself space to look at the build up to the conflict, hence his interpretation of Henry's address to his troops at Dale.

The anonymous writer would either have been told that Henry declared his intentions in this way, or it was a piece of literary licence. Even though the earliest extant copy of the Ballad dates to the mid-seventeenth century, the poem is believed to have been written some time between 1485 and 1495:-

> That was well seene att streames stray,
> At Milford haven, when he did appeare
> With all his Lords in Royall array
> He said to them that were with him weare
> Into England I am entered heare,
> My heritage is the land within,
> They shall me boldlye bring and beare
> And losose my life but I'll be King.
> (Anon: The Ballad of Bosworth Field, lines 49–56)

As darkness closed in Henry continued to address his soldiers, stressing the need for good behaviour on the march. He had no desire to annoy the people of Britain, of Wales in particular. He was coming as their saviour and had no truck with anti-social behaviour which would alienate everyone.

French troops in particular had a bad reputation for looting and wiping out the livestock of any area they passed through. This was the result of a long standing French policy of not providing sufficient rations for the soldiers, expecting them to forage off the land. Not here, Henry ordered, stealing or foraging would be punishable by death.

Henry also insisted that the men should occupy only the lodgings assigned to them by the harbinger. He had already sent out this harbinger, or official, who would operate in front of the army, finding food and lodgings for the men. Often they would have to bivouac out in the open but good food and drink, bought by the harbinger, should have made them comfortable wherever they were forced to lay their heads.

As Jasper, Philibert Chandee and the Earl of Oxford soon told Henry, more worrying than their potential for bad behaviour was the ability, and quality, of the French mercenaries. They were so poorly armed that Oxford and Jasper would have been loath to pitch them into a battle. Henry might talk of exemplary behaviour but many of them had no idea how to conduct themselves as soldiers. It was something Henry and his lieutenants would have to deal with later.

For the moment it was felt best to keep the French separate from the Welsh soldiers who would, hopefully, come flocking to his flag. Nobody wanted the new recruits to be influenced or infected by the truculent Frenchmen.

It is doubtful that Henry had much sleep that night. He would have been excited but wary, not knowing what lay ahead of him. He was up early the following morning, Monday 8 August, and was soon on the march, leaving Dale behind him:-

> From thence departing in the breake of day he went to Haverforde which ys a towne not ten myles from Dalley wher he was receavyd with great goodwill of all men.
>
> (Polydore Vergil, Books 23–25)

Haverfordwest, an important market town in the fifteenth century, was the first significant settlement Henry had encountered and it was crucial that the populace should be supportive. It would reassure him and confirm Jasper's oft-stated opinion that the Welsh would rise to join him.

Support from the people of Haverfordwest there certainly was, the populace happily welcoming the man they saw as one of their own. It was a justification of Jasper's much repeated words – he was not Sais, he was Welsh.

Perhaps the people of Haverfordwest were sensible in their welcome. The town castle, which had been strong enough to withstand a siege during the Glyndŵr rebellion in 1405, was now beginning to fall into disrepair. (Dillwyn Miles: *Castles of Pembrokeshire* p.17) It was not well garrisoned and if it had come to battle there was little doubt about who would have won.

Here in Haverfordwest Henry was joined by Arnold Butler, the same man who had accompanied him to Brittany all those years ago. He had since been returned to his native land on the orders of Duke Francis and had not seen Henry for fourteen years. He was living in the Pembroke area and made the trip across the Cleddau to meet his old friend.

Butler brought with him a body of troops, the first Welsh additions to the invading army. He also assured Henry that the whole of Pembrokeshire was behind him and that the nobility and gentry of the county would willingly give him their support – provided he was prepared to forgive them for anything they had done while Henry and Jasper were in exile in Brittany. Henry was no fool and immediately agreed.

Perhaps more importantly, Butler was a close friend and ally of Rhys ap Thomas. If Butler was now pledging him his allegiance, Henry thought, did that mean the reluctant Welsh leader was also considering his situation?

Henry remained concerned and unsure about the motives and loyalty of Rhys. It was a feeling that would not leave him for many days but now the words and actions of Butler were at least partly reassuring for him.

Chapter Six

The Long March

The appearance of Arnold Butler at Haverfordwest undoubtedly cheered Henry but it was not long before more worrying news wiped away any jubilation he might have felt. John Morgan, the same messenger who had brought him the news of Rhys ap Thomas's supposed defection before the fleet left Harfleur, suddenly reappeared on the scene. As Vergil wrote, the message now was very different, 'clene contrary to that he was certyfyd of in Normandy.' (Polydore Vergil, Books 23–25)

It seemed that Rhys was not yet prepared to defect to his cause. For the moment at least he remained in the service of King Richard.

Henry was dismayed at the news but was somewhat mollified by the fact that neither Rhys nor William Herbert, the Earl of Huntingdon, had yet moved against him. Herbert, son of his old custodian at Raglan Castle, controlled the majority of south east Wales and along with his brother Walter and Rhys ap Thomas was a major player in King Richard's defence of the region. Henry remained hopeful that the two men were simply biding their time, waiting to see how the Welsh reacted to his arrival. It was not much of a straw to cling to but it was all Henry had got.

The problem that now faced Henry was which route to take. With Rhys ap Thomas at or near Carmarthen, and William and Walter Herbert controlling the crossings of the Severn at Tewkesbury and Gloucester, it seemed that the direct route to London was denied him. Therefore he would march north and meet up with two potential allies, Thomas and William Stanley who controlled much of North Wales, before crossing into England somewhere near the town of Shrewsbury.

Henry immediately sent a message to his mother, Margaret Beaufort, and to the Stanleys and Lord Talbot, another possible ally, informing them of his intentions. He desired them to meet him at some point on the march before he swung south for London and the inevitable confrontation with Richard.

60

The journey would be hard going as the countryside in this part of Wales offered no easy route, only rugged and difficult walking. It would be something of an endurance test for his soldiers who, at the end of the march, would then face the prospect of a pitched battle. Nevertheless, unsure as he was about Rhys and the Herberts, Henry and his advisors (principally Jasper and the Earl of Oxford) felt there was no other option.

Henry Tudor did not stay long in Haverfordwest. He did pause long enough, however, for refreshments and for his scouts to report back. They now told him that Rhys ap Thomas had been in Carmarthen but had now left the town. His destination remained unknown, the scouts simply passing on the news that he had gone. Henry was worried – had Rhys left Carmarthen to join him or attack him? He had no way of knowing.

Having made his decision about the route, Henry crossed the Western Cleddau and left the town of Haverfordwest just a few hours after he had arrived. He was headed for Cardigan, then an important port and market town which lay on the coast 25 miles to the north.

Henry's route lay over the Preseli Mountains. As a mountain range the Preselis are not particularly high, being just 1,760ft at their summit, but they are invariably battered by winds off the Irish Sea. Coarse grass, bracken – or furze as it is known in Pembrokeshire – and jagged rocks litter the terrain. In 1485 the roads would have been poorly made and uneven, little more than cart tracks. Even in August it was a cold, inhospitable area with sudden rain squalls and mist regularly hammering in from the sea. This was the land that had given the builders of Stonehenge their precious blue stones, but it is doubtful that Henry and the marching soldiers either knew or cared.

Just 5 miles out from Haverfordwest, before the real hardships of the Preseli Mountains began, Henry called a halt, deciding to allow his men time to rest. It was a rest that was soon rudely broken, as Polydore Vergil was to later write:-

> The whyle the soldyers refreshyd themselves rumor was suddeynly spred through the whole camp thautor whereof was uncertane, that Gwalter Herbert and those who were in camp at the town of Carmardyne were at hand with an huge army.
>
> (Polydore Vergil, Books 23–25)

Men instantly grabbed their weapons and 'stood to' as a wave of fear ran through the camp. Henry and his lieutenants tried desperately to calm things down but it was not easy. Fear of the unknown was always greater than the reality. The source of the rumour was not clear but if Walter Herbert, younger brother of William, and Rhys ap Thomas really were at hand it looked more than likely that a battle would have to be fought within the next few hours.

Henry immediately despatched riders to find out if the rumours were true. The scouts soon reported back that everything was quiet and that there was no sign of the enemy. Henry's soldiers put down their weapons and lay back around their picket fires. They were relaxed once again. When, shortly afterwards, Gruffyd Rede from Carmarthen and John Morgan of Tredegar rode into the camp along with a band of soldiers – most welcome even if they were poorly equipped – the cause of the rumour was discovered. It had been a case of mistaken identity.

Rede and Morgan had been with Rhys ap Thomas in Carmarthen but had decided to throw in their lot with Henry. Along with Arnold Butler, the defection of the two men – both significant figures in Welsh society – began to convince Henry that his Uncle Jasper had been right. The Welsh would come to fight at his side.

Quite where Rhys ap Thomas stood was still unclear. According to the two new defectors he was now marching north, mirroring Henry's route but journeying along the spine of Wales and maintaining a safe distance from the invaders. How long he would continue to keep his distance nobody knew.

It seems that Henry somehow managed to open up lines of communication with Rhys. The two men remained in regular contact with each other throughout their respective marches. Perhaps Rede and Morgan were instrumental in establishing this contact, or maybe Arnold Butler, taking and delivering messages, but there is no firm evidence as to how it came about.

Henry knew that sooner or later he would have to fight against Richard. His claim to the throne was perhaps not as 'fraudulent' as N.M. Gwynne has suggested but it was, at best, fragile. There were members from the lineage of John of Gaunt still alive and ahead of him in the line of succession.

Henry's royal lineage came through his mother Margaret, a line that had been 'excluded from the throne by Act of Parliament' (N.M. Gwynne: *Gwynne's Kings and Queens*, p.170). It meant that if he was going to claim the throne the only way it could be justified was by right of conquest. That meant defeating and probably killing Richard in battle.

Other battles or skirmishes would probably have to be fought before Henry came face to face with the Yorkist king. The obvious candidates to oppose him were Rhys ap Thomas and Walter Herbert. By maintaining his contact with Rhys, Henry hoped that sooner or later he would come over to his side – as had already been hinted. Walter Herbert was a somewhat different matter.

On every step of his journey through Wales Henry feared an attack by Herbert. It never came. For some reason, known only to himself, Walter Herbert failed to move against him. Two of his chief lieutenants, Richard Griffith and Evan Morgan, did defect to Henry, but of Walter Herbert there was no sign either on the march or on the battlefield at Bosworth.

Henry and his troops spent their second night in Wales camped at the fifth milestone out from Haverfordwest on the road that snaked up over the mountains. After resting for the night the mood of the soldiers had brightened and early on the morning of Tuesday 9 August they set off on the next stage of their journey.

X X X

Now the hard marching really began. It is difficult to imagine the effort required and the back breaking-agony of the marching men, ploughing doggedly on for mile after mile in the sunshine and the rain or whatever the weather threw at them. The leaders, Henry, Jasper and the rest, would have had horses. The ordinary soldiers had no option but to walk.

In 1985, on the 500th anniversary of Henry's march to Bosworth, Peter Lewis, then Sheriff of Haverfordwest, emulated his feat by walking from Dale to the battlefield. It took him nine days of constant walking, covering approximately 31 miles each day. The walk left him exhausted:-

> I had roads. The soldiers in 1485 had mud. That march must have been something else. I carried a small haversack and Pat, my wife, would drive on ahead and find hotels and guest houses for the night. Back in 1485 they would have had to carry their tents and blankets and their weapons. At the end of each day I knew that Pat would be around the next corner with the car. Not the soldiers of Henry's army. They didn't have luxuries like a soft bed to sleep in at night; mostly they were out under the stars.

> I remember sitting in a pub in Tamworth, at the end of the
> walk, trying to pick up my pint from the table in front of me.
> I just couldn't grab it or hold it. I couldn't eat. Everything
> was impossible. I was physically and mentally exhausted.
> (Peter Lewis, conversation with author, April 2018)

Peter Lewis's exhaustion – he also got himself a split shin and blisters –
was after many months of training for the walk. Henry's men did not have
the luxury of such preparation and had, in fact, just spent several weeks
sitting idly on ships or waiting to board them. The march to Bosworth
Field must have been crippling. The fact that any of them made it remains
a miracle. The emotional or mental strain would have been every bit as
bad as the physical:-

> It was lonely up there on the hills. Every five or ten minutes
> a car would pass or speed towards me but mostly I was alone,
> staring out at the grass, the rocks and watching the buzzards
> and kestrels. Back in 1485 those soldiers would have seen
> nothing, no passing traffic. It must have been mind blowing.
> I know that by the end I was in poor shape. God knows what
> Henry's soldiers must have felt like.
> (Peter Lewis, April 2018)

Henry's route on the second day of the march took him across the Preseli
Mountains. They went through Bwlch-y-Gwynt (the Pass of the Wind)
and down to Fagwyr Llwyd just south of Cilgerran. Fagwyr Llwyd, now
long demolished, was then a large farmhouse standing just off the main
roadway. At the very least it probably gave Henry a roof over his head.

Here the soldiers made camp for the night with the sound of the River
Nevern tumbling and singing in their ears. It had been a walk of just over
15 miles, not long by the distances they were later to cover but the rugged
nature of the terrain had played havoc with the men's feet. Reassured
by the fact that the Preseli Mountains were now behind them and that
somewhat gentler terrain awaited them, the men still needed a welcoming
camp site.

As they walked or rested alongside rivers like the Nevern comradeship
grew. Adversity and expectation combined to weld the disparate groups
of men into a united force. Jasper and Oxford knew how men reacted to

situations like this and knew also the value of a leader to give a sense of purpose to the mission. Slowly but surely Henry was growing into that role.

The next day's march took Henry and his troops to Cardigan. In the fifteenth century Cardigan was a walled town, standing high above the river and dominated by its castle at the south western corner. Henry's troops crossed the River Teifi and cautiously approached the town and castle. They need not have worried, there seems to have been little, if any, resistance from the castle which, like Dale, was poorly garrisoned. Henry appeared before it and the castle soon capitulated without a fight.

It had been a short march, not that anybody was complaining. Henry, Oxford and Jasper had expected conflict at the end of it but they had encountered only a warm welcome and, despite the short nature of the day, they decided to pause for a while. Local tradition says that Henry rested at the Three Mariners Inn.

From Cardigan Henry sent out his own Commission of Array, similar in many respects to those issued by Richard. Just like Richard's missive, Henry's Commission began with the words 'By the king.' The document was intended for the gentry and landed classes but was a strong appeal to all of the people of Wales. Henry understood, said the Commission, that they had been oppressed by the depredations of Edward I and by the harsh laws imposed on them by Henry IV following the rebellion of Owain Glyndŵr. Henry had come to deliver them, he said, from 'the miserable servitudes as they have piteously long stand in'.

Henry was clearly finding his feet and now felt confident enough to appeal to his fellow countrymen. The Commission could obviously not be impressed with the country's Great Seal which was still with King Richard in Nottingham, but the imprint of Henry's ring was attached in wax onto the letter. Perhaps more importantly there was also the phrase that failure to respond to the Commission of Array would be met with 'grievous displeasure'. It seemed that even Henry Tudor was not above making threats if he felt the situation demanded it.

The following day Henry left Cardigan and continued with his march northwards. After 14 miles the army paused at Ffynonnendewi where Henry supposedly drank water from the well. They then resumed their journey. After a long march of over 20 miles the force stopped for the night in the parish of Llandysillio-gogo.

Where Henry spent his night is unclear but it is possible that he took his rest at Neuadd, the home of Dafydd ap Ieuan. Certainly Henry later presented Dafydd with the Hirlas Horn, an elaborate drinking vessel set on a silver stand. Embossed with various insignia, including a Welsh dragon and a greyhound which was the mark of the Woodville family, the horn was a valuable and remarkable piece of art.

Chris Skidmore in his book on the beginnings of the Tudor dynasty makes the interesting speculation that not all of Henry's army might have marched with him from Pembrokeshire. The bulk of the force, he suggests, could well have remained on board ship and come ashore here in Llandysillio-gogo, a few miles south of Newquay:-

> A small fleet may have traced the Welsh coastline, allowing more troops to disembark once Henry's advance party had reached this next location.
>
> (Skidmore: Bosworth: *Birth of the Tudors* p.239)

It is speculation and would depend on the willingness of Guillaume de Casenove to risk his ships by remaining off the Welsh coast. It does remain a possibility but without written proof there is no way such a suggestion can be verified.

Meanwhile, the long march continued. After resting at the ancient manor house of Llanilar close to the church of St Hilary, a bare 4 miles south of Aberystwyth, on Friday 12 August Henry's army came within shouting distance of the main town in the area. Aberystwyth Castle was held in the name of Lord Ferrers, one of Richard's strongest and most ardent supporters, and as Henry's troops approached it was clear that, unlike Dale and Cardigan, this fortress was not prepared to surrender, at least not without a fight.

The garrison, however, was not strong and it seems that the castle was taken after a brief skirmish or assault. It is not clear how many casualties were sustained, if any, but the lack of information on this point seems to indicate that if there were any injuries or deaths the numbers must have been very small indeed.

Richard had always thought that the Earl of Richmond's invading force was diminutive in size and of little consequence. Polydore Vergil wrote that the king had a very poor opinion of Henry and of his forces, believing that, 'He was utterly unfurnyshyd and feeble in all thinges.' (Polydore Vergil, Books 23–25)

Richard might have had a poor opinion of Henry and his ability, but he had the utmost faith in his own standing as a military leader. He had no doubt that his ability, his experience and skill as a warrior, combined with superior numbers, would surely give him the edge. Confident he may have been, but Henry's unimpeded journey through Wales and, in particular, his seizure of castles such as Cardigan and Aberystwyth must have given the king some cause for concern.

Richard would have liked nothing more than to assemble his troops and immediately set off to confront Henry. That was his instinct but all the advice from his friends and nobles entreated him to stand his ground. They had time and could choose the place to fight. It did not stop the king wondering about the ease with which Henry seemed to be making his way through Wales.

He was not the only one who was worried, albeit for different reasons. Henry still remained unclear about the intentions of Rhys ap Thomas and the further north he went, the more vulnerable he became. The *Life of Sir Rhys* later recorded that he deliberately kept his plans secret, deliberately not declaring for Henry:—

> Rumour indeede, Rice himself, out of policie, had caused to be blowne abroad, to hoodwinke the tyrant, until he were in his full strength. And this his devise, he acquainted the Earle withall, at their first meeting.
>
> (Ralph A. Griffiths: *Sir Rhys ap Thomas and his Family* p.226)

The reasons for Rhys's indecision at this time – if, indeed, indecision it was – remain unclear. The Life of Sir Rhys was written many years later and was always intended to put Rhys in the best possible light so the claim that his ambivalence was a deliberate ploy has to be taken with a large amount of caution. The most honest response would be that he was a political animal and was clearly weighing up where his best chances of survival lay.

Richard had been making dire threats to the nobility of the country, ordering them to come to Nottingham to fight at his side. Anyone who failed to appear could be subject to punishments that included the loss of his goods 'his possessions and his life'.

Threatening letters went out to men like the Duke of Norfolk, the Stanleys and Henry Percy, Earl of Northumberland. In many cases the threats worked and resulted in several additions to the king's forces. Not with everyone, however, and rumours within the court adamantly stated that far too many of the Lords were delaying their arrival in the hope that the campaign and the battle would be over before they arrived.

One tried and trusted way of circumventing any problem like this was to take and hold hostages. Any transgression or failure to support the king would then result in the death of the captives. It was an old technique but it was one that Richard now decided to employ.

In particular Richard had grave suspicions about Henry's father-in-law Thomas Stanley, the third husband of Margaret Beaufort. The link between the Stanleys, Margaret and Henry was far too powerful to ignore and Richard knew he had to go carefully.

When Stanley, the king's steward, asked for permission to leave court and return to his estates Richard agreed – but only if his son, George, Lord Strange, remained behind as his deputy. Nobody was under any illusions; Richard might call it deputising for his father but everyone knew Lord Strange was lodged with him as a hostage.

Despite being captured while attempting to escape the castle at Nottingham, Lord Strange was retaken and, probably under torture, soon told Richard that his father was planning to join Henry. He then wrote to his father – again, probably under duress – reminding him that his life was in jeopardy if he did not come to the king's side.

The plan was not totally successful. In fact it actually backfired on the king. Sir Thomas Stanley, far from rushing to support Richard, remained firmly neutral. His younger brother William was more open in his disgust and rebuked the king for such un-knightly behaviour. He promptly declared for Henry, promising to bring down dire punishment on Richard's head for daring to lay hands on his innocent nephew.

Richard – and Henry who was also beginning to question the motives and actions of his father-in-law – was right to have doubts about Thomas Stanley. By 1485 he had been in the service of three different kings, Lancastrian and Yorkist alike. He had been the chamberlain of Henry VI and a steward for Edward IV.

Richard did not trust him one inch, even though Stanley was now once again steward of the royal household and a man seemingly in good favour with the new king. Richard was familiar enough with the art of double dealing and knew that Lord Thomas was also a master craftsman in this area.

Stanley's skill at political manoeuvring and vacillation had seen him regularly remain aloof from conflict, verbal and physical, until he was absolutely certain who would win – at which point he would throw in his lot with the potential victor. If that made him distrusted at court at least his soldiers liked him. They felt that he would not send them needlessly to their deaths but wait until the opportune moment.

Holding important men like Lord Strange captive or as hostage was a recognised tactic and a similar problem affected Rhys ap Thomas. Richard demanded that his son Gruffydd ap Rhys ap Thomas be sent to him, again as surety against any change of heart that Rhys might suddenly have.

It has always been assumed that Gruffydd was duly sent to the king but some sources now state that Rhys refused to comply with the king's wishes because the boy was only 3 or 4 years of age and that this delivery of his son into the king's custody did not actually occur. Either way, the threat had been made and Rhys knew that in Richard's mind he was a marked man.

As Henry marched northwards Rhys followed his track, taking a more southerly route but remaining between him and London. It was faintly alarming for Henry as he remained unclear about Rhys's intentions.

His way lay through Llandovery, Brecon and across the mountains of Mid-Wales. He was effectively shadowing Henry, but while contact between the two men seems to have been fairly regular and reasonably cordial there was still no indication which way Rhys would jump. He could have as easily attacked the Tudor army as he could have joined it.

As Rhys marched he, like Henry, gathered Welshmen into his force which now numbered as many as 2–3,000. There were even women and children attaching themselves to him and he was eventually forced to reduce the number of people in his company, which had become rather unmanageable.

Somewhat reluctantly – after all, these people had pledged themselves to him and put their lives at risk – he decided to send some home and leave 500 as a rear guard under the command of his brothers and his elder son. It left him with a force of between 1,500 and 2,000 eager and confident troops, all well-equipped and mounted.

Henry was now in possession of Aberystwyth but the persistent rumours that Rhys ap Thomas would remain a faithful vassal to King Richard were still there. And day and night those rumours troubled him. Regardless of this, Henry knew that he had marched northwards for long enough. There was no turning back; it was time to make for England.

Chapter Seven

Into England

On 13 August 1485, Henry left Aberystwyth and made the 23 mile march along the Dyfi Estuary to Machynlleth. He had no further interest or aims in Wales. The country of his birth had served its purpose and from now on his direction and his eyes were set firmly to the east.

Henry spent the night at Mathafarn, the home of poet, preacher and part-time prophet Dafydd Llwyd. The house lay some 5 or 6 miles outside the town and offered Henry a comfortable lodging. One legend about his stay at the house, possibly apocryphal but indicative of the uncertainty of the time is probably worth repeating.

During the evening Henry asked the poet to use his skills and prophesise about his future. In particular he wanted to know whether or not he would be victorious in the coming battle. Dafydd, nervous and unsure about what to say, asked to sleep on the matter. During the night his wife advised him to proclaim a victory for the Tudor earl – after all, if he became king he would probably reward them; if he failed he would be dead and unable to trouble them. The next day Dafydd provided a positive response and Henry went happily on his way.

The words of Dafydd's wife proved to be both accurate and productive. In the wake of his later victory Henry, now King Henry VII rewarded the soothsayer for his prophesy by making him Esquire of the Body. There is no record of any gift being made to Dafydd's wife.

The validity of the story hinges on one question – was Henry superstitious? Of course he was; most people were at that time, including Richard III, and Henry would probably have held similar views. It was a literal age. God was a living being, in man's image, while witches and warlocks roamed the planet to practice their art. Omens, good or bad, were a crucial part of life and Henry needed every bit of luck he could find. Why would he not believe in prophesy and fortune telling?

Henry's uncertainty throughout the march – in particular about the intentions of Rhys ap Thomas and the Stanleys – might have led him to seek consolation from a renowned soothsayer. The story remains speculation, yet again, but with just enough links to reality to be true.

Machynlleth was a significant stop for Henry. Here Owain Glyndŵr, the last true Prince of Wales – even if he was self-proclaimed – had set up his government, calling a Welsh Parliament that sat in splendour in a house in the main street. It was a symbolic moment for the man who was now claiming to be the champion of the browbeaten Welsh people.

While in Machynlleth Henry took the opportunity to send out more appeals to the nobles and landowners who stood between him and Richard, urging them to join him in 'the recovery of the crown of our realm to us of right appertaining'. Messages to his mother and friends like the Stanleys were also despatched, letting them know he was about to cross into England. He did not expect a reply from the Stanleys, not at this stage, and so the lack of reply did not worry him unduly – at least not more than normal. Besides, Henry now had something more cheerful to contemplate.

It was while he was resting and writing letters at Machynlleth that Henry was finally told Rhys ap Thomas had made his decision. He was now willing to join him. His support, however, would come at a price:-

> Henry promysyd to Richerd Thomas the perpetuall lyetenantship of Wales, so that he would come under his obedience, which afterward when he had obtanyed the kingdom he gave lyberally.
>
> (Polydore Vergil, Books 23–25)

As far as Henry was concerned the price was cheap. Despite his repeated proclamations, his banners and emblems on which he proudly displayed Welsh emblems, he had no real love for Wales, other than it being his place of birth. In fact, Henry would never enter the country again once he had become king. England had always been his target, England and the crown. By granting Rhys the lieutenancy or governorship of Wales he knew that, whatever was happening in London or in any other part of his kingdom, his western flank would be safe.

The long march began again on 15 August. This time they took to the hills, staying well clear of the roads and tramping along the valley of the Severn towards Newtown. They did not pause in the town but marched on, through the pass of Bwlch-y-Fedwen to their destination. This was the mansion house of Dolarddyn outside Castle Caereinion. While his troops settled down for the night in the grounds, Henry spent the evening inside the house with yet another warm and pleasant roof over his head.

The following day, 16 August, the army moved on. The previous day's march had been a crippling 30-mile journey but today Henry had a much shorter trip in mind. It was just 6 miles to the market town of Welshpool – but they did not stop there. A few miles beyond the town lay Mynydd Digoll (the Long Mountain), not much more than a steep hill but with a flat summit and wonderful views over the Welsh borderland into England.

It was here that Henry was finally joined by Rhys ap Thomas. Polydore Vergil reported the fateful meeting in a languid style that, even now, belies the significance of the event:-

> Richard Thomas (Rhys ap Thomas) met by the way with a great bande of soldiers, and with assuryd promysse of loyaltie yealdyd himself to his protection.
>
> (Polydore Vergil, Books 23–25)

It must have been a wonderfully reassuring sight for Henry, watching Rhys approach, banners flying, horses snorting and men cheering. With great pomp and ceremony Rhys then climbed to the summit of the Long Mountain where Henry was waiting. He brought with him between 1,500 and 2,000 soldiers and now as they and Henry's other troops stood and watched, Rhys ap Thomas finally bent his knee and pledged his allegiance to the Tudor cause.

The arrival of Rhys lifted a huge weight off Henry's shoulders. He had worried for weeks about the man's loyalty and even after receiving the message at Machynlleth he would not be totally sure about Rhys's intentions until they had finally met. Talk, Henry thought, was one thing, action was something entirely different.

As if the arrival of Rhys ap Thomas was not enough, that night more Welsh landowners and gentry joined Henry's force. They brought with them soldiers and fresh provisions. A group of Welsh drovers, with their cattle also joined Henry at this point, providing the grateful soldiers with vast quantities of beef, and Henry's confidence soared. Things were going exactly to plan.

X X X

From the top of the Long Mountain Henry and his lieutenants – now including Rhys ap Thomas – had a fine view of England where the town of Shrewsbury lay waiting in the sunshine. This, as Henry had planned, was the spot he intended to cross the border and lead his men out of Wales.

Henry's idea was to cross the River Severn by Shrewsbury's Welsh Bridge, but when he approached the town he was surprised to find the gates firmly locked with the portcullis down. Despite his repeated protestations that he intended no harm to the people or to the town itself the gates remained closed.

Thomas Mitton, the town bailiff, was clear that his loyalty was reserved only for Richard – hardly surprising as the king had granted him the lordship of Cawes and various monetary awards for his support during the recent rebellion of the Duke of Buckingham. Henry was shaken. This was the first setback he had encountered and rather than risk a violent confrontation he decided to withdraw. He and the army fell back to the village of Forton, 3 miles away, to consider the next move. His men camped on the heath while Henry spent the night in the house of a man called Hugh Fortune.

The following morning Mitton changed his mind and told Henry's messenger that he would open the gates and let the forces of the Earl of Richmond pass through the town. Something had influenced the bailiff during the night. Possibly it was the arrival in the town of Sir Richard Corbet and nearly 1,000 soldiers, on their way to join Henry's army – Corbet was, after all, the son-in-law of Lord Thomas Stanley who held sway as the main landowner in the area.

There is also a legend that Mitton remained firm in his refusal until Lord Stanley's instructions to open the gates were given to him. They were, apparently, written on paper which was tied to a large stone and thrown over the wall into the town; it was one way of getting the orders across. Having received these, the town bailiff had no option but to open the gates.

Mitton had apparently sworn an oath to the king, stating that he would defend Shrewsbury to the death. Do not be afraid, he had declared to Richard, Henry would only enter the town over his belly. Myth and reality here mix again!

It is the old story – Thomas Mitton supposedly lay on the ground and Henry stepped over his prostrate body as he was reported to have done with Rhys at Mill Bay or Mullock Bridge, thereby preserving the sanctity of his oath. The tale, like the one about Rhys, is almost certainly apocryphal, and fear of Lord Stanley's wrath was more likely to be behind the bailiff's change of heart.

The Earl of Oxford, aristocratic and unforgiving to the end, was furious at what he saw as Mitton's lack of respect and threatened to behead him. Only the personal intervention of Henry saved the man's life.

The townspeople, apparently, took a different view on things. They were probably thinking about soldiers' spending money in their shops and ale houses but, even so, they were warm in their welcome. The Life of Sir Rhys ap Thomas later commented that Henry was well received in the town, speaking of:-

> the streets being strewed with herbes and flowers, and their doors adorned with greene boughs in testimonie of a true hartie reception.
>
> (Ralph A. Griffiths: *Sir Rhys ap Thomas and his Family* p.226)

While the story of Henry stepping over Mitton's body is more than likely false, there must be some degree of truth in the account of the welcome he received from the ordinary people of the town. Accounts for the period show that a sum of £4 4*s* 10*d* was paid by the town towards expenses and for wages of men who had been subsequently hired as soldiers for Henry. The accounts were signed by Thomas Mitton.

When Richard heard that the Earl of Richmond had passed through Shrewsbury and crossed the Severn he was furious. He had been concerned when Lord Strange had admitted his father's intention to declare for Henry but, so far, he had done nothing about the vacillating nobleman.

He had been angry at the behaviour of the younger Stanley, Sir William, who was clearly using the Commissions of Array to raise troops for Henry. As a consequence Richard had already declared him a traitor. It was no more than he deserved, the king felt.

But this was a different matter altogether, this was something far more serious. Henry Tudor was across the border and now in England.

Richard had intended to set out to confront the rival for his throne on 16 August. Attack was always his first response to any problem but now, instead of venturing out to challenge Henry, he retired for the night to his hunting lodge at Bestwood, a few miles outside Nottingham. It was a move that showed a degree of uncertainty normally alien to Richard. His indecision might have been due to over confidence or, at the other end of the spectrum, a degree of trepidation. Whatever might have caused it, such delay was totally out of character for the king and was ultimately to prove catastrophic.

It was late in the evening of 17 August when the king returned to Nottingham. He had not reached his chamber before he was met by the news that Henry was across the Severn. According to Vergil he flew into 'a fervent rage'. (Polydore Vergil, Book 25) Angry, disappointed and faintly alarmed, the one thing the king now knew – he could afford to delay no longer.

He immediately sent out his scouts, scurriers as they were known, to pinpoint the exact location of Henry and his army, and made final preparations to leave the city. His army was already huge, by some accounts as many as 15,000 men from all corners of his kingdom, now crowded into the streets and taverns of Nottingham.

X X X

Thomas Stanley had left his castle and estates at Lathom on Monday 15 August and headed for Newcastle-under-Lyme. His brother William was already in the field camped 20 or 30 miles north of Shrewsbury, but soon he too was on the march. William was aiming for Nantwich and was gathering soldiers as he went. Meanwhile Henry had crossed the Severn on the eighteenth of the month and made camp on the open land outside the small town of Newport. There, during the evening, Lord Gilbert Talbot and 500 fully armed soldiers joined him – more welcome additions to Henry's army.

The following day, 19 August, Henry moved again, this time heading northwards to Stafford. It seemed like a strange move to make, particularly as he had already declared that London was his destination, but his reason for heading north was actually quite simple. He had come to Stafford to meet with William Stanley. It was a brief and not entirely satisfactory meeting, however, and it left Henry puzzled and perplexed.

Yet again Henry was faced by indecision and lack of clear promises from the men he had counted on for support. He had spent days worrying about Rhys ap Thomas but now, when that issue appeared to be settled, the attitude of the Stanleys – not just comrades in arms but his in-laws – was unsettling. While William pledged his personal allegiance he was not prepared to commit his brother to the coming fight and, by the same token, his own men also would be held back.

No matter how hard he tried, Henry could not get William to pledge anything more than Lord Stanley's friendship. As for where he was proposing to stand in the coming battle, both Thomas and William Stanley remained unwilling to commit themselves. The attitude was an enigma that puzzled Henry and gave him more concerns that he really did not want. Despite statements of support, decisions on how he would conduct himself in the battle would have to come from Thomas himself.

Following their brief meeting William Stanley returned to Stone while Henry turned south. He was back with his original plan, intending to join the old Roman road of Watling Street, a good straight highway that would take him directly to London. With Richard still in the Midlands, Henry's intention was to by-pass him, reach London and declare himself king. He would then, as the new sovereign, gather more support and turn to deal with the dethroned monarch.

That evening Henry camped outside Lichfield. That was where Richards's scurriers located him and reported back to the king. Some of the scouts remained in the vicinity as they later reported to Richard on the welcome the Tudor earl was given in the town the following day.

On 20 August Henry entered the town where he was received with a warm and enthusiastic wave of support. Thomas Stanley had been there just a few days before and had undoubtedly 'warmed up' the local population. He might not yet have declared for Henry, but his confusing behaviour continued. In so many aspects of his behaviour and attitude he seemed to be Henry's man, even though he refused to just come out and say it. Preparing the people of Lichfield for the coming of the earl was just one thing that he did to help his son-in-law.

There is even a possibility that Henry was received by the townspeople, not as the Earl of Richmond, but as the king. Whether or not that was down to the words of Thomas Stanley is not known. If this story of a royal reception is true it was slightly presumptuous of the ordinary men and women, the dignitaries and the clergy of Lichfield, who all turned out to greet him. Presumptuous it may have been but at least it showed that Lord Stanley had not joined Richard – at least not yet.

Stanley had deliberately left Lichfield before Henry arrived and moved on to Atherstone alongside Watling Street. It was a position that put him directly between Henry and Richard where he could, as he soon informed the king, block Henry's route to the south and in particular to London. Whatever he or his brother had told Henry, he was still keeping his options open, particularly as Richard still had Lord Strange, his son, in custody:-

He fearyd the danger that King Richerd might doo his son
and so dyd enclyne as yeat to nether partie.
(Polydore Vergil, Book 25)

If Henry's welcome in Lichfield had been spectacular, Richard's departure from Nottingham certainly matched, and maybe even surpassed, it. With banners flapping in the wind, with horses rearing and kicking, with trumpets and drums sounding, the moment of departure was announced to the city.

Thousands of soldiers moved easily out into open country. They were an arresting sight, column after column of marching men with the king at their head. Most of them were mounted, not that they intended to fight that way. Horses would get the soldiers to the battlefield fresh and ready to fight. The horses would then be quartered and the fighting would, in the main, take place on foot. Only the king and the nobles would fight on horseback.

Once out in the open the army deployed into a massive square defensive formation, a square battle as it was known, with Richard in the centre. He rode a great white horse and seemed to those who watched to be calm and at ease. He was confident, yes, but the front that he presented to the people hid a degree of apprehension and uncertainty.

By evening Richard's great array of soldiers was at Leicester. Dusk was blending with darkness when the king's army joined with the troops of the Earl of Norfolk who were already in the town waiting for Richard's arrival. The combined armies now constituted a significant fighting force. It was one of the largest military gatherings ever seen in the Midlands, outnumbering Henry's troops by at least two to one. Commanded by an experienced and capable leader there was every reason to think that it would sweep everything before it – and Richard's ability as a soldier had never been in doubt:-

> In feates of armes, and matters of chilalrie, to give the devil
> his dewe, he was nothing inferior to the best.
> (Ralph A. Griffiths, p.228)

Even so, Richard was concerned that several of his noblemen and supporters had not yet arrived. Apart from the Stanleys he was still waiting on the Earl of Northumberland and Robert Brackenbury who was bringing with him ordnance from the Tower of London. Both of them, along with more troops, arrived early the next morning, calming any nerves that Richard may have felt.

Richard supposedly spent the night at an inn or tavern in Leicester called The White Boar. He had brought with him his own bed which was erected in an upstairs room. He also brought vast amounts of 'treasure', which were carried into his bedroom.

The presence of both the treasure and the bed was nothing unusual for medieval monarchs who, when they decamped from London and its palaces, invariably needed the succour of personal possessions to keep them comfortable. It might have been inconvenient for his servants but it was to be expected of King Richard.

Combat was not far away, both sides inching closer and closer to each other by the day. Tensions remained high as for both Henry and Richard the moment of decision was at hand. Both had belief in themselves and in their causes, but both of them knew that tomorrow or the next day battle would be joined and there could be only one winner.

Spies or scurriers from both sides were out as Henry broke camp and moved his forces towards Tamworth, a distance of some 7 or 8 miles. The scurriers would have been intelligent men with military experience and knowledge of things like terrain. If they knew the area they were covering, that would have been an extra bonus.

When Henry's scouts returned their reports were not good. The scurriers had swiftly sought out news of the enemy, sweeping like ants across the terrain and returning to inform him that King Richard was close at hand. More importantly, their estimates of the number of troops at his disposal were beyond anything Henry had thought possible. Richard's army was enormous, they reported, a huge body of men, at least 10,000 and all of them ready to fight at a moment's notice.

There was no doubt that Richard's army was a significant force, but that was almost despite his Commissions of Array rather than because of them. His unpopularity in the country had become increasingly marked and was reflected in the somewhat lacklustre response to his call.

It was not always the fault of the nobles, as Richard undoubtedly believed. The Duke of Norfolk and his son Surrey, for example, had intended to bring 1,000 men but they quickly discovered that recruitment was not easy. When they mustered at Bury on 16 August they soon realised that 1,000 was a figure way beyond them.

Norfolk's lands had been previously owned and governed by the Earl of Oxford, a man who had been popular with his tenants and the populace, but had been stripped of his possessions by the king and was now standing alongside Henry. When it came to mustering for his successor Norfolk – and, ultimately, for the king – the two Yorkist noblemen soon found that many men had simply slipped away and remained hidden until matters had come to a conclusion.

With so many failures to respond to the Commissions of Array, the fact that Richard managed to assemble an army of well over 10,000 remains amazing. Had he been a popular monarch, someone well thought of and admired, the response would have been very different. Henry did not know how lucky he had been.

The Tudor army spent the night of 20 August close to Tamworth Castle but strangely – and worryingly for Jasper Tudor, for the Earl of Oxford and for new adherents to the company like Rhys ap Thomas and Gilbert Talbot – Henry was not with them. He had disappeared at some stage during the march to Tamworth.

Chapter Eight

Drawing the Battle Lines

A continual flow of defectors was still seeping out from Richard's camp and coming to join Henry. That should have given Henry heart, but now that the final reckoning was close, the Tudor earl was consumed by doubt, by confusion and by more than a little fear. It was not the first time he had felt like this on his journey from France, across Wales and into England.

His scurriers had reported back and the news was not reassuring. The army gathered together by his enemy, they now told him, was somewhere in the region of 12,000 men, perhaps more. The huge number of troops at Richard's disposal was terrifying, particularly for someone like Henry who had very little experience of war.

Once again he began to doubt his ability to command soldiers in battle and, significantly, to face Richard in what was bound to be a fight to the death. This time, however, the worries were like a gigantic rock rolling and grinding in his belly.

Just as troubling as his own self-doubt was the continuing reluctance of Thomas Stanley to commit himself to the cause. Henry had counted on his father-in-law, his battle plans indicating that he needed Stanley and his troops very badly indeed. If he was being honest to himself he needed every soldier he could lay his hands on.

Henry had journeyed through Wales as if on a tidal wave of popularity. Sometimes it had seemed too easy, that journey – a royal progress, almost, when it had appeared as if it was his destiny to ride the unstoppable wave to victory. Now, he began to have second thoughts, not just about the coming conflict but the whole enterprise. As he marched, and as the scurriers' disquieting reports came steadily in, he realised he needed time to think things through. He needed to be alone.

As his army marched on towards Tamworth, Henry deliberately hung back. At the time nobody thought much about it; their concerns and thoughts were on the coming battle and the part they would play. Soon Henry and his small escort of twenty mounted men lost sight of the troops in the gathering gloom.

As Henry prevaricated and dawdled away the last of the evening sunshine the army marched on without him. Soon it was dark and Henry realised that he had lost touch with his troops. In Vergil's later account Henry and his escort wandered around for some time, trying to regain contact, before stumbling into a small village where they stayed the night.

Whether or not Henry was genuinely lost, he had achieved his aim. He was alone and with no one there to bother him he could think about his problems. In particular he could go over in his mind the ways in which he would confront Richard when the battle came.

If Henry was unsure and concerned, the same could be said for his troops. The disappearance of their leader caused panic to spread throughout the ranks. Had he deserted them, had he been captured by Richard's men? For the rank and file who had pledged themselves to his cause, and for the noblemen who had put their lives, their families and their titles in jeopardy, it was a long sleepless night.

It was with an enormous sense of relief that Jasper Tudor and the Earl of Oxford saw Henry approaching the camp early the following morning:-

> Henry the next day after, in the gray of the morning, returnyd
> to the hoste, excusing himselfe that he was not deceavyd in
> the way, but had withdrawen from the camp of set purpose
> to receave some good newys of certane of his secret frindes.
>
> (Polydore Vergil, Book 25)

Vergil says no more about the incident. He certainly never discloses who Henry's secret friends might have been or the nature of the 'good newys'. Henry himself said nothing about his evening of wandering the countryside and by the morning of 21 August seems to have recovered his composure and his courage.

He was aided in this by further defections from King Richard's camp. Renowned warriors like Brian Sandford, Simon Digby and John Savage joined him, each of them bringing with him large numbers of troops.

Before long Henry was back to his normal self and the escapade of the previous night was consigned to memory.

There may well have been secret friends but the reality of the situation was that Henry – always thoughtful and self-critical, often unsure of himself – must have been close to throwing in his hand and running. The fact that he chose instead to rejoin his command speaks volumes about his courage – to doubt is one thing, to face that doubt and overcome it is something else entirely.

The disappearance of Henry Tudor that night is rarely spoken about. Indeed, Polydore Vergil was the only chronicler to even mention it – and his information had to have come from Henry himself. Whether or not Henry thought his story about meeting secret friends had been believed it shows the courage of the man to even mention it to Vergil years after the incident when it could so easily have been forgotten.

However, Henry's temporary defection is an essential part of the story and the legend of the march to Bosworth Field. It shows Henry in a human light, beset by worries and fears that would have destroyed many ordinary men – a far cry from the dour and miserly figure that we normally associate with Henry VII.

X X X

According to Chris Skidmore there may have been skirmishing on the night of 20/21 August, small engagements between the forces of Lord Stanley and Richard's advance guard (Skidmore, p.173). Both Stanley and Richard now had significant bodies of troops in the area and initial probing from either side would have been entirely possible.

That said, Stanley had still not declared his true intentions and had only recently told the king that the position he had taken up was crucial if Henry was to be stopped from marching down Watling Street to the capital. How Richard received his explanation is not known, but at that stage Stanley had no reason to expect an attack from Richard – displeasure, yes; attack, no.

Despite this, the two Stanleys were certainly expecting some sort of attack on the morning of 21 August and drew up their forces accordingly. Lord Thomas did not welcome the idea of such an attack. An assault, if it came from the king, would certainly have forced his hand and made him finally declare for Henry. Stanley, the master of trickery and vacillation, was not ready, even at this late hour, to make such a statement.

His troops were still in battle order when, with a blast of trumpets, Henry Tudor suddenly arrived on the scene. It was the first meeting of Henry and Lord Stanley and they came together, by chance as much as by design, at the Merevale Priory outside the village of Atherstone. The meeting seems to have been positive with both men greeting each other warmly and laying out their proposed dispositions should battle with the king be joined the following day.

Battle was something that Henry now certainly had in mind. When their discussion ended he left Stanley and guided his forces away from the main road to a position that was near the town of Market Bosworth. The exact location was decided by men from the area, men with local knowledge, but was probably somewhere in the vicinity of Witherley, Atterton and Fenny Drayton villages. It was not a stone's throw from Stanley's camp at Atherstone.

Richard was told of Henry's position early on that Sunday and immediately understood that the Tudor earl was ready to stand and fight. His first response was to mount his horse and ride out to inspect his troops. They were an impressive sight but even as he studied them with his practised soldier's eye, Richard was pensive.

Although the nobility of England was well represented, including men like the Duke of Norfolk and the earls of Surrey and Northumberland, one significant figure was still missing – Lord Thomas Stanley. It was not just Stanley who was missing. The reluctant nobleman had 6,000 troops under his command, men who would have been more than useful to Richard.

It was too late now to worry unduly. He would concern himself with Stanley in due course and, anyway, he had more than enough soldiers to deal with Henry Tudor. Concerned but not afraid, the king prepared himself for battle.

His next move, the obvious one, was to leave the town of Leicester and take up position close to Henry, ready for the morning. He needed to be in place early, in order to have the choice of position on the battlefield. He rode out from the town at the head of his troops, the crown of England on his head and his White Boar standard billowing in the breeze.

It was just a short march before Richard made camp at Sutton Cheney, close to Ambion Hill. From the top of the hill the marshy expanse known as Redemore lay below him and away in the distance he would have been able to pick out the camp of the waiting Tudors. Compared to his own mighty host, Henry's army seemed pitifully small.

Richard had chosen his position well, commanding the high ground from where he could observe the dispositions of his enemy. The slope would also have given him a decided advantage if it came to battle at this spot. A charge, momentum carrying riders and footmen alike down the slope to hit the enemy lines at speed, would have been a fearsome sight. It was not something that Henry's tiny force looked even remotely like being able to withstand.

As night fell Richard's soldiers lit their camp fires and cooked whatever food they had available. They expected to sleep in the open or under hastily built canvas awnings. Richard spent the night in rather more luxurious surroundings.

The royal tent was quickly pitched and hung with tapestries to give it an air of splendour. Rich carpets covered the floor while silks and golden ornaments filled the tent, everything to make the king feel warm and at home. And yet, despite the trouble taken for his comfort, Richard passed a troubled night:-

> Yt ys reportyd that King Richerd had that night a terrible dreame, for he thowght in his slepe that he saw horrible ymages as yt wer of evell spyrtes haunting evydently abowt him – and they wold not let him rest.
>
> (Polydore Vergil, Book 25)

In this superstitious age such a dream was, Richard felt, an omen. But he kept his thoughts to himself and although, by some accounts, seeming particularly white and gaunt, he still managed to appear in front of his troops that morning as a man full of confidence. The soldiers themselves would have made note of his appearance and taken pride in their king and in his ability as a leader.

Polydore Vergil was later to seize on the sleepless night of the king and make political capital out of it: 'Yt was no dreame but a conscience guilte of haynous offences.' (Polydore Vergil, Book 25). He was, of course, writing for Henry long years after the battle and was keen to show Richard in as bad a light as possible.

Richard was up with the dawn on the morning of 22 August, somewhere about 5.30. He had barely slept and his restless early movement inside the tent caused a few problems. To begin with he wanted to hear Mass – a private Mass rather than the traditional one that would be celebrated with and in front of the troops. According to the 'Crowland Chronicle', a virtually contemporary account of the battle, Richard was out of luck.

Unfortunately for him the chaplains were not yet prepared and were caught out by the early hour. Nobody could lay their hands on the bread and wine needed for the ceremony which left Richard fuming at the incompetence of his chaplains. If the spiritual members of Richard's entourage were unprepared so, too, were the royal cooks – breakfast was not ready either. (Crowland Chronicle, 1486)

Richard, despite his evil reputation, was an intensely religious man. Superstition and the power of the church were combined in this religious age and before a battle such as the one about to take place Richard would have wanted to ensure that God was on his side. The fact that he was asking for a personal Mass before battle shows how important religion and spiritual belief were to him. He wanted the protection of his God and would have been troubled by the failure of the chaplains to deliver the Host, far more than he would have been by the loss of his breakfast.

A few miles away Henry Tudor was also making his final arrangements for the challenge ahead. He, too, had been awake for some time, worrying, thinking, sending messages to people like Lord Stanley and ensuring that his dispositions were correct. He might not be as skilled as Richard but he was eager to make up some of the deficit with proper and appropriate preparations.

It is hard to know what Henry and Richard were thinking at this time but we can guess. As with all men before battle they would have been assailed by thoughts of mortality. Both of them would have hoped and prayed, literally, for success, but Henry in particular would have been anxious. If he lost today it would inevitably mean his death – and the death of the Tudor/Lancastrian dream.

Henry knew that this whole enterprise was a gamble, one he had always considered worth taking. But the further he got into the march and the closer it came to the final battle the more his anxiety grew. Old soldiers like Jasper and Oxford were used to 'pre-battle nerves'. For Henry this was a totally new experience.

Richard would have been confident but troubled by the omens that had plagued him over the past twenty-four hours. Things like his terrifying nightmare and the failure of the chaplains to provide the bread and wine for his Mass were huge and important issues that must have been whirling through the brain of this hugely religious and superstitious man.

During the night several more men had slipped away from his army to join Henry, including one of his trusted Commissioners of Array. The repeated haemorrhaging of men and equipment at this late stage of the campaign may not have been significant as far as troop numbers were concerned but it would have undoubtedly added to the king's discontent.

It was not just in Richard's camp that darkness shielded significant movements. The night-time hours had also seen much movement on the other side of the field. At some stage of the night Thomas Stanley had arrived on the field of battle, taking up a position to the side of the forthcoming combat zone at a spot that was effectively halfway between the two armies.

The cynical response of men like Jasper Tudor would have been that from there he could turn and join either Henry or the king, as the mood took him. Jasper, Rhys ap Thomas and the others might fume and curse, hint darkly at the motives and movements of Henry's father-in-law, but there was nothing they could do.

It was clear to everyone that Stanley was still keeping his options open, right to the end of the affair. Henry, for the moment, seemed unperturbed. Whatever agreement had been decided on at Merevale Priory the day before had reassured him of Stanley's intentions. We will never know for sure what had been decided but the discussion probably included Thomas's position on the battlefield and the plan of action for the day.

Presumably operating to the terms of the verbal agreement reached at Merevale, as the first streaks of daylight began to punch holes in the eastern sky Henry sent a messenger to Stanley, requesting that if he was ready he should now position his troops in the battle line.

Henry had already given Lord Stanley command of the vanguard and was expecting him to take his place at the head of the troops. Stanley's reply, however, immediately wiped away all of Henry's new-found confidence and plunged him once more into deep depression.

Despite what had been agreed the previous day – the exact terms of which will remain unclear for ever – Stanley's reply was that he would indeed join the battle line. But he would only do it when Henry himself was there and actively engaged with the enemy.

The news was devastating; it smashed into Henry like a thunderbolt for it meant that he would now have to go into battle without Stanley's 6,000 soldiers. The promise that Stanley would join the fray when Henry was committed meant absolutely nothing. He was already seriously outnumbered but this sudden and unexpected news effectively reduced his odds even further. Richard's force was now more numerically superior than he had ever expected.

Some sources state that Stanley was not totally impartial, however, and that even as he waited, he noted the size of the two forces. He did endeavour to help Henry:-

> Recognising that Henry's forces were too small to combat Richard's army, he sent Sir Robert Tunstall, Sir John Savage, Sir Hugh Percivall and Sir Humphrey Stanley to join Henry's vanguard.
>
> (Skidmore, Page 286)

They were all good, well-seasoned soldiers, Humphrey Stanley being the youngest brother of Lord Thomas, but that was scant consolation for Henry. He needed large numbers of troops and he needed them quickly. He needed the 6,000 men that the Stanleys had mustered and he needed the vital skill and experience of their two leaders.

What sort of game was Thomas Stanley playing, Henry wondered? Did he really intend to join him or was it all an elaborate set up by the king and the Stanleys?

Even Sir William Stanley, a man previously so positive in his personal support for Henry and so condemnatory of the king, was that morning refusing to commit himself. Instead he waited alongside his elder brother, proving that the Stanley propensity for 'sitting on the fence' was confined not just to Thomas, but was a family trait.

Despite the fact that Richard had declared William a traitor the younger Stanley was clearly unwilling to make what could have easily been a fatal move, not just for himself but for his whole family. Whichever side won he would have to do some quick political manoeuvring, but that was nothing new; the Stanleys were well used to playing that particular game.

As the moment of destiny drew steadily closer Thomas and William sat astride their horses at the front of their divisions – battles as they were known – observing the manoeuvring of the two opposing armies but remaining uncommitted and aloof.

Henry and his advisors had immediately realised that Stanley's decision to hold back until battle was joined could well be the death knell of their hopes. Richard's superior numbers would surely overwhelm them in the early stages and then Stanley would throw in his lot with the king. It was too late now to withdraw. They were committed to the fight, whatever the numbers, whatever the odds.

As dawn finally broke on the morning of the battle it was clear to everyone that Henry Tudor and his supporters appeared to be in serious difficulties.

Chapter Nine

Bosworth Field

The Battle of Bosworth Field was one of the most significant clashes of armed men in the history of Britain. Yet for years it was underplayed and all but ignored. The battle was poorly recorded and reported on by contemporary writers; most of the accounts were put together in the years after the Tudor dynasty had become firmly established. The view of such writers was, inevitably, somewhat biased. That has affected our knowledge and understanding of what went on. Even now, knowledge of the battle remains sketchy.

One of the principal primary sources of information is the poem, 'The Ballad of Bosworth Field.' It is a detailed and intriguing account of the lead up to the battle and the actual fighting. But there are a number of difficulties with its provenance.

Firstly, the poem was written probably within two or three years of the battle, but the version that we see today dates from the middle of the seventeenth century. That is the earliest known extant version, the original copies from the time of the battle having long disappeared. The poem is probably not much different from the earlier examples but there is always an element of doubt.

Secondly, general consensus indicates that due to the repeated lavish praise of the two Stanley brothers found in the poem, the anonymous writer was probably a member of either Lord Thomas or Sir William's entourage. That, of course, means that the author cannot have seen every phase and detail of the battle. On the contrary, he would have seen very little as Sir William Stanley did not enter into the fray until the last moments.

In order to write the comprehensive account that we see today, the author must either have talked to other soldiers who managed to see a great deal more than him, or he used literary licence. Either is possible and does not detract from the value of the Ballad as an historical record. It might not be great poetry, but at least the writer does not sacrifice the truth in favour of a good rhyme.

The battle, which began early on the morning of 22 August 1485, lasted for two hours and resulted in a victory for Henry Tudor and the Lancastrian forces. The Plantagenet dynasty died with King Richard, the line of Tudor monarchs began. Beyond that lies a great deal of conjecture and informed guesswork, combined with what little information has survived.

Troop numbers along with casualty figures from the engagement are largely hypothetical and vary according to who was telling the story. Over the last twenty years even the location of the battle has been questioned and the site repositioned. Strange as that may seem, it fits in with the way Bosworth Field was considered by early Tudor historians. The battle was fought and won, Henry was on the throne, and nothing else mattered.

Whichever view you take, the old site for the battle or the new one, there remain many over lapping details which could and probably did occur at whichever site you care to hang your hat. So, the traditional view first!

X X X

Early in the morning of 22 August, King Richard drew up his troops in line of battle. The original thinking, and for years the perceived wisdom, was that he did this on the flat plateau at the summit of Ambion Hill. His army was split into the traditional formation of three divisions or, as they were always known, battles.

Richard took command of the central or main battle. It comprised a force of 3,000 infantry, all experienced and well-armed. The king was accompanied by his personal guard, the knights of the body as they were known, and by members of his household.

The Duke of Norfolk, along with Sir Robert Brackenbury, was on the right flank with the vanguard, his spearmen protecting large bodies of archers and artillery. According to the anonymous author of 'The Ballad of Bosworth Field', Richard had 140 serpentines or cannon chained together in a row. They had been drawn largely from the armoury at the Tower of London and brought to the king's army by Brackenbury.

There were also a number of bombards helping to make up Richard's artillery force. The bombards were smaller than, and not as accurate as, the serpentines but they made a lot more noise and smoke. That was considered a great advantage.

Archaeological digs have recently uncovered thirty-four cannon balls from the area, more than have been found on any other medieval battlefield in Europe, which seems to confirm the huge number of guns available to the Yorkists. Some are solid, others more flexible at their core so that when they landed they would shower the target with early versions of shrapnel.

The Earl of Northumberland took command of the left flank or the rear guard with 3,000 of his troops being mounted. According to some accounts the strength of Northumberland's full battle was in the region of 10,000 men, but they were drawn up some way behind Richard's centre. That would have made communications between the king and the earl quite difficult while attempting to make sudden manoeuvres in the heat of battle would have been, to say the least, far from easy.

Despite the location of Northumberland's rear guard Richard's forces seem to have been drawn up in the most advantageous of positions. He and Norfolk were both of them experienced and capable commanders and would have taken care to ensure their battles were well situated to take advantage of the terrain. As well as the advantage of the slope, the Yorkists had the sun and the wind behind them. This would cause problems for the Lancastrians who would have to squint and narrow their eyes in order to see properly. The wind would also assist in the flight of arrows and quickly disperse the smoke from the cannons, blowing it towards the enemy.

That morning, as far as the eye could see Richard's soldiers were spread across the hill top. Packed together in their three battles they appeared to be a formidable mass of men, armed with swords, halberds, axes and pikes. With the archers and artillery on their flank it seemed, at first glance, to be an unbeatable force.

Richard's biggest problem, however, was not quantity, but the thorny issue of quality. Most of his rank-and-file troops had been assembled after their lords or town sheriffs had received the Commissions of Array from the king. That made them effectively forced labour. Their military training and service in times of war were limited. When confronted by soldiers like Henry's, many of whom had experience of battles on the continent and, as far as the Welsh in particular were concerned, had immense faith in their cause, the natural instinct of these unwilling recruits would have been to throw down their weapons and run.

In order to prevent this Richard ordered that the conscripted men should be backed by experienced pikemen in their rear. That, he felt, should be sufficient to prevent them breaking and fleeing. As a secondary precaution Richard's scurriers were also ordered to move along their flanks in order to keep them in line and moving forward. It may have sounded effective but it was hardly the best way to send inexperienced men into battle.

Soldiers on both sides would have been armed with a variety of different weapons. Of course there were swords and spears but almost every foot soldier also carried a rondel, a small sharp dagger which was used to finish off knights when they had been knocked from their horses. The halberd, a cross between a spear and a battle axe, was another popular weapon and was probably the implement used to batter Richard to death. Maces, bows and, in particular, battle hammers would also have been in common use.

Many of the conscripts were poorly armed and they certainly lacked the plate or chain mail armour of the professional soldiers. Those professionals would have worn brigandines over their armour, cloth jackets with metal plates riveted to the cloth, along with metal helmets or helms. They would have been well protected, unlike the reluctant masses that probably went into battle cloaked only by leather, heavy wool or corduroy working jackets.

Willing or reluctant, Richard's army that morning probably numbered about 15,000 men. Seeing them gathered together on the ridge must have given the king a huge boost after his sleepless night and the evil omens that had troubled him. When he gazed at Henry's small force assembled on the flat ground below him his confidence would have leapt even further. This, he must have felt, would be a contest that would be over very soon.

According to some sources Henry's army numbered 7,000. Even that would have been a gross over-estimation. A more accurate figure, as supplied by Vergil – and therefore passed on to the writer by Henry himself – would have been around 5,000. As a relative novice in the art of war Henry had delegated tactical command of the army to the more experienced Earl of Oxford while he retired to the right rear flank of his force.

Acknowledging that the Lancastrian army was outnumbered three to one, Oxford decided not to split them into the three traditional battles but keep the troops together as one mass. Such a move was an accepted way of going into battle against superior numbers as Oxford knew well. He had studied tactics as well as being experienced in the art of warfare and had fought, won and lost many times during the Wars of the Roses.

With soldiers clustering around their banners – Oxford had decreed that no soldier should stray more than 10ft from his unit's standard – it meant that the army, while presenting a united front, was really made up of individual groups of men pulled together by comradeship and intensity of purpose. It was to be an important factor in the hours ahead.

Gilbert Talbot had charge of the right wing of Henry's army, John Savage the left. Rhys ap Tudor, his black-cloaked Welsh warriors eager to begin the fight, was with Talbot on the right. Oxford himself took up position at the front of the line along with the invaluable archers. Horsemen guarded the flanks. The whereabouts of Jasper Tudor at this time remains unknown but it is probable that he remained with Henry in the rear. Whatever the result of the battle, Henry Tudor had to be kept safe.

The two Stanleys continued to remain apart, standing on their hill to the right of Henry's army, left of Richard's. Their troops were drawn up in battle order, ready to intervene at a moment's notice. Nobody yet knew, however, in whose favour they would intervene.

The Earl of Oxford understood only too well the issue of troop morale. The imposing sight of Richard's soldiers drawn up in massed ranks along the hill top could be devastating on the courage and steadfastness of purpose among his outnumbered soldiers. He determined that he would not stay long in this position. Henry was clear, however, that he was intending to speak to the troops before they advanced.

With a wry look towards the inactive Stanleys, Henry's speech to the army that morning included a reference to 'doubtful friends'. Then he turned and went back to his position at the rear. Oxford watched him go and then ordered the army to move forward. And so the battle began.

X X X

Richard was caught out by the sudden movement of the Lancastrian army but like Henry, he still had time to make the customary pre-battle address to his troops. The two speeches were hugely different and reflected the character and the emotions of the two principals.

Henry in his address to his men had reminded the soldiers of the justness of their cause and promised gifts, titles and positions of honour to those who performed well. God, he reminded them, was on their side:-

> But he of his bountiful goodnesse will this daie send us triumphant victorie, and a luckie journie over our proud enemies and arrogant adversaries.
>
> (Holinshed: Chronicles of England, Scotland and Ireland, Book 6, 1577)

Richard resorted to threats. If they should lose today, he said, Henry would destroy the houses, homes and families of all those who had fought for the king. The message was simple – fight well or else! He did temporise a little, telling his troops that:-

> Victorie consisteth not in multitude but in manlinesse. Wherefore let all feare be set aside.
>
> (Holinshed, Book 6, 1577)

Richard also found time to send a message to Lord Stanley. He would execute Lord Strange, he stated, if the Stanleys did not now engage. Thomas Stanley's reply was simple – 'I have other sons.' Richard immediately ordered Strange to be brought to him. In light of his father's unfeeling response it was time, he said, for his execution. His officers, Sir William Harrington in particular, intervened, reminding the king that the battle was about to begin. Beheading Lord Strange could come later when, with any luck, they could add the two Stanleys to the death toll. Richard agreed. By such miniscule margins Lord Strange's life was saved.

Stanley might have sent a negative response to the king but even so he still did not move. He and his brother simply sat apart from the battle, watching the progress of the two sides. Both Henry and Richard must have glared in his direction and cursed him for his inactivity.

Oxford's unexpected advance saw him flanking the marsh at the foot of the hill, keeping it on his right hand and using it as protection. Seeing the enemy movement Richard immediately ordered the Earl of Norfolk to charge forward and attack. Archers from both sides loosed their missiles but the result seems to have been negligible. 'The Ballad of Bosworth Field' comments on the use of archers and artillery at this stage:-

Then they countered together sad and sore.
Archers they let sharp arrows fly,
They shot guns both fell and far,
Bows and yews bended did be.
(Anon: The Ballad of Bosworth Field)

The cannons opened fire, terrifying men and horses with their noise and smoke. Oxford, however, managed to avoid much of the artillery fire by wheeling left and then hurling his troops against Norfolk's flank. Fifteenth-century serpentines were heavy and it would have taken valuable time to swing them around and aim them at Oxford's new line of advance.

The battle now became a hand-to-hand melee, archers and footmen alike hacking at each other with swords, daggers and clubs. The manoeuvring was over, now it was a case of kill the man ahead of you before he killed you.

An anonymous poem written at the time of the battle seems to sum up the confrontation as men sweated and cursed under the morning sun. The noise of metal clashing against metal, men screaming as they died, would have been appalling:-

Foot by foot and point by point
Arms sound on arms, and man assails man.
(Anon, fifteenth-century verse, copy held by the Author)

The fight was furious and reflected not just the animosity between the Yorkists and the Lancastrians, but also the hatred that existed between Oxford and Norfolk. Everybody knew that Oxford's titles and lands had been stripped from him by the king and presented to Norfolk. Whatever the outcome of the battle, this was a chance of revenge for the Earl of Oxford.

After a period of furious fighting, there was a lull in the action when Oxford pulled back his troops to regroup. Both sides stood leaning on their weapons and panting from their exertions. The respite was only temporary and it was not long before Oxford ordered his men forward again.

During the lull the earl had sent a message to Gilbert Talbot and Rhys ap Thomas on the right flank. They should, Oxford ordered, form themselves into a wedge formation, charge Richard's main battle and smash a hole in the enemy formation, thus isolating the Earl of Norfolk from the rest of the Yorkist army.

The wedge, not dissimilar from the later column attack of the French armies during the Napoleonic Wars, was a highly effective battering ram against tightly packed linear formations like the one Richard had assembled. Used properly it could be a battle-winning tactic.

Norfolk could not ignore the wedge and was forced to turn to his left to deal with it. This, combined with renewed fierce attacks by Oxford, managed to turn the flank of Norfolk's battle and enabled the Lancastrian army to move around behind them.

It was a stunning blow and a clever manoeuvre by Oxford. It meant that the Yorkists on Norfolk's wing were now being attacked from all sides and, more importantly, they had lost the advantage of the elements. Now they would have to fight with the sun in their eyes. The battle was not one for the faint hearted:-

> Brands rang on basinets high,
> Battle axes fast on helms did light.
> There died many a doughty knight'
> There under foot can they thring;
> Thus they fought with main and might.
>
> (Anon: The Ballad of Bosworth Field)

Oxford's attack was relentless and after a few minutes many of the Yorkists, most of them the conscripted men, simply turned on their heels and ran. Walter Devereux, Lord Ferrers, one of Norfolk's senior commanders, was killed and Richard, watching events unfold, realised it was time for the reserve. Urgently he signalled to the Earl of Northumberland to put his battle into the fray. There was no response and to the king's horror Northumberland's reserve failed to materialise.

It has never been entirely clear whether Northumberland chose to remain inactive, or if the narrow terrain and his position half-a-mile to the rear of the main battle line prevented him moving his troops. Either way, the reserve did not come to Norfolk's aid and now the position of the men in the vanguard became perilous.

Some accounts, written well after the battle, state that Northumberland had reached an understanding with Henry before the action actually began. They had, after all, been friendly as adolescents and Henry Percy, Earl of Northumberland, had no love for Richard. Many believe that the northern earl now turned his men on Richard. Such an action was highly unlikely and has never been verified.

An understanding between the two men was possible but it is far more likely that Northumberland, like the Stanleys, was simply biding his time and waiting to see how events unfolded. He would have witnessed the disaster that had befallen Norfolk's vanguard and realised that things were swinging Henry's way. From now on it was simply a matter of choosing his time.

As Northumberland hesitated it became obvious that Norfolk's battered troops had finally had enough. First they faltered, and then fell back. Finally, they broke and ran, their rout accompanied by the news of their leader's death.

How Norfolk actually met his end is not entirely clear although one account states that it came after a face-to-face encounter with Oxford. Norfolk wounded the Lancastrian, his sword glancing off Oxford's helmet and slicing into his upper arm. Oxford hit back, splitting open his opponent's helmet. At that point Norfolk was struck by an arrow in the face and died.

An alternative version has Norfolk fleeing to a windmill on a nearby hill. Here he was apprehended by John Savage who took both him and his son, the Earl of Surrey, into captivity. According to this account Norfolk, on the orders of Henry and the Earl of Oxford, was executed soon afterwards.

However his death occurred, Norfolk was dead and his battle, Richard's vanguard, was utterly routed. This was hardly what Richard had expected and he fumed about treachery and betrayal. Knowing that the battle was virtually lost, his senior officers advised him to flee and even managed to find a fast horse for his use. Richard probably did consider running but his concept of knightly chivalry, on the battlefield at least, remained strong. He would stay and fight.

The writer of 'The Ballad of Bosworth Field' goes into some detail about Richard's men trying to persuade him to leave the field:-

> Here is thy horse at thy hand, ready.
> Another day thou may worship win
> And for to reigne with royalty
> To weare the crowne and be our King.
>
> (Anon: The Ballad of Bosworth Field)

Richard's comment on the matter was brave and fearless. Nobody has ever doubted Richard's personal courage and his reply has gone down in folklore, becoming synonymous with his final minutes: 'God forbid that I retreat one step. I will either win the battle as a king or die as one.'

And at that moment fate presented him with one last chance. Far below him Richard suddenly picked out the standard and the form of Henry Tudor. He was some distance from the main force and guarded only by a small body of horsemen. Richard's military skill quickly asserted itself and his practiced eye saw that Henry was open to a swift attack. Rashly, Richard decided that he would end it all there and then. He placed his crown on his head, positioning it over his helmet, and led a charge down the hill towards his hated Tudor enemy.

Earlier in the day Richard had recognised Henry's standard with its bold dragon emblem but at that stage the Tudor earl was too far to the rear to contemplate a charge. Now, with the success of Oxford's manoeuvres, Henry had followed the advance and was much closer to the front. He was, as Richard realised, suddenly vulnerable:-

> He strick his horse with the spurres, and runneth out from thone syde without the vanwardes agynst him. Henry perceavyd King Richerd come upon him – he receavyd him with great corage.
>
> (Vergil, Book 25)

How many knights Richard took with him in the charge is yet another fact that has become lost. Some accounts say it was as many as 800, others that he was accompanied only by his household staff and a few close friends. If the latter is true it would have been a brave but foolhardy attempt to end the battle. He would surely have taken a reasonable force with him in such a critical enterprise.

The charge was dynamic and desperate, the shock of mounted men – fully armoured and moving at pace – smashing like a tidal wave through the small reserve of pikemen that Oxford had left to protect Henry's front. The pikemen did, however, absorb the impetus of the charge, slowing Richard and gaining valuable time for Henry who gathered his bodyguards around him and prepared to face the advancing King. Henry, like Richard, must have realised that this was the crux – or as he might have had it, the brunt – of the battle.

According to a group of French mercenaries who were close by, Henry took refuge among their number where he presented a less obvious target.

Now fighting on foot, Henry and his guard battled manfully just to keep Richard at bay but they were under severe pressure and it began to look as if the king might just achieve his aim.

Richard fought magnificently. A slight man of no great size or strength, he was a skilled swordsman who excelled with all the weapons available to knights at that time. He was also fearless. He cut down Henry's standard bearer, Sir William Brandon, and then managed to unhorse the huge figure of John Cheyne. Standing 6ft 8in tall – far above the average height for men in those days – Cheyne made an impressive barrier between the two rivals for the throne. Size meant nothing to Richard when the fury of battle was on him and he smashed Cheyne to the ground with the blunt end of a broken lance:-

> He matchyd also with John Cheney, a man of muche fortytude far exceeding the common sort, who encountered with him as he cam, but the king with great force drove him to the grownd.
>
> (Vergil, Book 25)

At that moment the Stanleys made their move. From his hilltop Sir William noticed Oxford's victory over on the left, but he also saw the action around Henry and watched as the earl's standard bearer went down. The Earl of Richmond was in danger. If he was ever going to declare for Henry, now was the time. He immediately charged into the melee, hurling his men against Richard's flank.

It was a timely intervention. Richard was moving steadily closer and closer to Henry, whose men were now 'almost owt of hope of victory' (Vergil, Book 25). With the arrival of Sir William Stanley, however, Richard was suddenly outnumbered and was pressed back a hundred yards. He was now on the edge of the marsh and his horse lost its footing in the mire. Richard was thrown to the ground as the horse tumbled into the mud and slime.

It was a crucial moment, the incident probably giving Shakespeare his famous line in *Richard III*: 'A horse, a horse, my kingdom for a horse.' It is doubtful if Richard ever said anything of the sort, he would have been too determined to get back into the action and destroy Henry. And now he battled forward once again.

Richard's standard bearer, Sir Percival Thirwall, was hacked down, losing both of his legs but keeping the king's standard erect and flying until he was eventually killed. James Harrington and Richard Ratcliffe were also killed as Richard battled forward once again.

He came within a sword's length of his target before finding himself alone and surrounded by enemy soldiers. Still fighting, he was battered to the ground, most of the blows falling on his head. His chinstrap was broken or cut and his helmet dislodged. The blows from halberds and swords continued, one being so violent that part of his basinet was driven into his skull. The rear part of his head was hacked off but the death blow was probably a sword or dagger thrust up into his brain.

Later examination of Richard's skeleton, after it was discovered in the famous car park in Leicester, showed that he suffered ten wounds, eight of them to his skull. Who delivered the final blow, like so much else in the story, remains a matter of conjecture.

Welsh tradition says that it was Rhys ap Thomas who administered the fatal sword thrust after a fearsome one-to-one encounter with the king. Certainly many poems were written by the Welsh bards, praising Rhys for his deed. However, like so many Welsh bardic efforts, the poems need to be read with a degree of caution. Then, before and after, the real art of the bard was praising the subject, something that was a great deal more important than telling the truth.

The Life of Sir Rhys, written many years after both Rhys and King Henry were dead, followed the same formula as the traditional Welsh poets and acclaimed Rhys as the king's executioner. The anonymous writer added, as proof, the fact that Henry ever after called Sir Rhys by the name Father Rice – which proves absolutely nothing.

The Life, as with the bardic poems, is not a work of fiction but a clever mingling of truth and fantasy. It is simply a case of sieving out the obsequious 'flannel'. As Ralph Griffith states in his Introduction to the republished work about Rhys and his family 'The Life deserves to be treated with cautious respect rather than scepticism.' (Griffiths, Page XVI)

Another version bestows the honour on a soldier by the name of Rhys ap Maredudd, sometimes known as Rhys Fawr (Great Rhys in English). Yet another candidate was a man by the name of Robert Woodshawe. Polydore Vergil who, by reason of his conversations with Henry, should have known, but he contents himself with a simple statement that praises Richard's bravery and never mentions the name of the man who finally put Richard out of his misery:-

> King Richerd alone was killyd fyghting manfully in the thickhest presse of his enemyes.
>
> (Vergil, Book 25)

At the end of the day it hardly matters. Richard was battered by so many blows – which apparently continued after he was confirmed dead – that any one of a dozen men could have inflicted the fatal wound. One thing is clear, however, Henry and Richard did not come face to face to fight the decisive contest, as depicted by Shakespeare and many others. That confrontation, so desired by Richard, so strenuously avoided by the Lancastrians, remains a figment of writers' imagination.

As news of Richard's death spread across the battlefield his army rapidly disintegrated. Most of the defeated soldiers fled, many more threw down their arms and surrendered. According to Vergil they had suffered about 1,000 casualties, a figure that is more than likely accurate given the nature of the combat. Henry's men, on the other hand, sustained approximately 100 dead.

Henry, with the battle ended, took himself to a hill near the village of Stoke Golding. The hill was later renamed Crown Hill, although there is evidence that it had been called that in ancient times, and it was from there that he addressed his troops, praising their courage and strength, promising them great rewards in the days ahead. His soldiers responded with loud shouts, proclaiming him their new king.

As if to cap the moment one of the Stanleys – again there has been considerable debate about which Stanley it was – placed the circlet that Richard had worn into battle on the head of Henry Tudor with the words 'I make you King of England.' The cynical response might be right place, right time!

Sir William had found the crown on the battlefield. It was never, as legend declared found in a hawthorn bush, even though a circlet of hawthorn was afterwards taken to be part of the Tudor emblem. William, the younger of the two Stanleys, may have found the crown but he probably passed it to Thomas, head of the family, to present to the new king, as would be fitting.

Whoever carried out the 'crowning', it was on the battlefield that Henry had made himself king and it was on the battlefield that his victory was first acknowledged.

With the battle over, Henry's first action was to make arrangements for the dead. The bodies were brought to St James's Church in Dadlington where they were prepared for burial. Nobles and men of position would have been taken back to their homes for burial. The rank and file would have been buried close to the battlefield, probably in mass graves in or around the churchyard at Dadlington.

Richard, however, was denied any immediate rest. Stripped naked with his hands tied he was slung across the back of a horse, hands and head hanging down on one side, legs and feet on the other. His privy parts – as one writer declared – were fully on show. The body was then taken to Leicester where the corpse was put on public display, supposedly to confirm that he was actually dead.

There were precedents for such treatment of vanquished warriors. Edward IV, for example, had caused the bodies of Warwick the Kingmaker and his brother Montague to be displayed for three days on the steps of St Pauls after the Battle of Barnet in 1471. Modern sensibilities cannot help delving into the deeper psychological motives behind such display. As far as Richard III was concerned it was the ultimate humiliation for a man who had prided himself on his knightly values but had slipped from his pedestal into the role of usurper, regicide and tyrant.

X X X

That is the traditional view of the Battle of Bosworth Field. There is now another, slightly different version. Many of the finer details about the action will be largely the same whichever version you choose to believe. Differences, where they occur, mainly concern the area or location of the battle.

The original positioning of the battle at the foot of Ambion Hill was accepted for many years as a true and accurate judgement. It sprang from a book written at the end of the eighteenth century, siting the battle to have taken place on Ambion Hill.

Many years later historian Daniel Williams was commissioned by Leicester County Council and identified the land at the foot of the hill as the probable site. A Battlefield Heritage Centre was built on the field of battle in the 1970s, close to what is known as Richard's Well, where the last Yorkist king supposedly drank on the day of the battle. He may have done but the location of the battle is, in all probability, wrong.

Geological surveys on behalf of the Battlefields Trust have now concluded that the land to the south and east of Ambion Hill, Redemore as it was known, was not marsh but solid ground in the fifteenth century. This is contrary to the accustomed theory that at the time of the battle it was marshland.

Redemore is an ancient Saxon word meaning reedy marsh but was a term that was also used to describe the area alongside the actual marsh itself. With the story of the battle depending so much on the presence of just such a marsh on Henry's right flank it is easy to see why the first identifications placed the battle here – as long as you believe that in 1485 this was marshland.

And yet we are now told that the area below Ambion Hill was not marshy at all. The name, therefore, could refer to the land alongside another nearby marsh, if such a thing could be discovered.

Archaeological work by Glenn Foarde between 2005 and 2009 has now suggested that the battle was fought some 3km southwest of Ambion Hill; 3km is not a great distance and the new site of the battle would have been easily reached from Richard's camp.

According to Foarde it was apparently fought on either side of the old Fenn Lane Roman road, close to Fenn Lane Farm and near to the villages of Dadlington and Stoke Golding. Here there was both a marsh (Fenn Hole) and a hill, perhaps not as high as Ambion but still a significant slope.

Foarde was extending and developing earlier work by Peter Foss which had revealed the existence of several fenn holes or marshes in the area around the boundaries of Dadlington, Stoke (as it was then called) and Upton. The wrong original identification of the battle site becomes more of a possibility and almost certainly derives from the poor recording of the event at the time of Henry's victory.

The suggested new site for the battle makes some degree of sense. To begin with there is the issue of the bodies of the dead. These were apparently removed from the battlefield to St James's Church in Dadlington, far closer to the new site than it is to Ambion Hill.

Logistically, the transporting of bodies – after having been engaged in a pitched battle where you fought and thrashed around for your life – would have been an unpleasant, backbreaking task. It did not matter how much you might have wanted to show respect to those who had perished, which Henry certainly did, burial duty was a task that no soldier wanted to draw. So the closer the bodies to the graveyards, the less work it would have been for the men!

The naming of battles has never been precise and this one was first known as the Battle of Redemore. It was also sometimes known as Brownheath and sometimes Sandeford. Only twenty-five years after 1485 did it get its final name, the Battle of Bosworth or, as it is more usually known, Bosworth Field, after the most significant town in the area.

None of the names are particularly apposite, Redemore meaning no more than a marshy area; Brownheath is exactly what it says, a brown or uncultivated piece of land; Sandeford, the name originally used by Henry, simply means a place of battle. Even Bosworth Field seems out of place – Bosworth, after which it is named, is located several miles away from the battle site.

Apart from the land in front of Ambion Hill being solid ground, Glenn Foarde uncovered several more significant reasons for re-siting the battlefield.

The discovery of many lead round shot and cannon balls on the new site was fairly convincing factual evidence. Both Henry and Richard used artillery during the battle, Richard probably far more than his opponent. Lead shot and solid cannon balls would have been spread over a wide range, particularly after centuries of ploughing and cultivation but their discovery here, close to the now long-vanished Fenn Hole, is compelling.

One of the versions of Norfolk's capture and subsequent death has him fleeing to a windmill situated on top of a hill. No such windmill existed in the area of Ambion Hill, but one did stand on a hill top close to the village of Dadlington.

This windmill was apparently later demolished and the materials sold. There is no modern memory of the windmill but the fact that records show it did exist at the time of Bosworth Field would fit in with the suggested new site for the battle.

More significant still, however, was the discovery of several artefacts on or close to the new site. In particular there was the uncovering of a small silver-gilt badge depicting a boar – the boar, of course, being Richard's personal emblem. It was exactly what archaeologists and historians would have hoped and wanted to find on a battlefield.

This badge or ornament, Foarde believes, was worn by one of Richard's knights who made the final charge with his king, and the place of its discovery, on the edge of what had been the marsh, was significant. It could be close to the spot where Richard fell.

The badge, which is finely wrought and designed, obviously belonged to a nobleman or someone of status and could well have been lost in the final moments of the confrontation when the fighting was at its fiercest. Who knows, it might even have been worn by Richard himself.

The discovery of a broken pommel or handle from a sword, close to where the badge was found, seems to indicate that serious hand-to-hand fighting had taken place here alongside the marsh. This would fit in with our understanding of Richard's final moments.

If Foarde's theory is correct it does not detract from our understanding of how the battle was fought and the progress of events over that furious two hour period. The manoeuvring would have been exactly the same, as would the moment when battle was joined.

If the new theory is to be believed, Richard assembled his troops on a slight ridge to the east of Fox Covert Lane. In front of him was the medieval marsh of Fenn Hole which has now disappeared. This would fit in with our understanding of the battle and with the writings of sixteenth century chronicler Raphael Holinshed:-

> Between both armies there was a great marsh then but at this present, by reason of ditches cast, it is growne to be firme ground.
>
> (Holinshed: Chronicles, 1577)

Henry would have approached the battlefield along the old Roman road and deployed at the foot of the ridge. The Stanleys waited just to the south. That left them near to the high ground that was later renamed Crown Hill – again, much closer to the new suggestion for the battle site.

The two sites are not dissimilar and the battle was probably fought very much as we have always believed – a hill or ridge for Richard's troops to assemble, marshland at its base. If Foarde's suggestion is to be believed, the only difference is that it took place just a few kilometres southwest of the original siting.

Chapter Ten

After Battle

There does not seem to have been much, if any, looting of bodies and equipment after the battle. Such things were not exactly expected in warfare but everyone knew it often happened once the fighting was over. Clothing, jewellery, weapons, everything was fair game to the scavengers. Not, it seems, after Bosworth Field.

The battle was fought in what was then a remote and rural part of Leicestershire, which may have deterred many from raking through the debris of battle. And yet locals from Dadlington and the other villages in the area are known to have watched proceedings from the church tower.

Perhaps Henry's care for the bodies prevented any indiscriminate pillaging. Or maybe it was the influence of the Earl of Oxford, who had already experienced the unfortunate results of indiscriminate pillaging. He undoubtedly retained the memory, unpleasant as it might have been.

Oxford's troops had begun looting during the Battle of Barnet when they should have been concentrating on defeating the enemy. By the time Oxford got them in control again it was too late and the Lancastrians duly lost. Whether or not the influence of Henry and Oxford had any effect on the after battle dealings of the local populace remains an imponderable, but the presence of soldiers on the battlefield may have reduced the opportunities.

Sir William Stanley was allowed to keep a huge proportion of the spoils from Bosworth Field. These he stored in Holt Castle and, together with his huge estates in North Wales, became very rich. (Williams, Page 24) Knowing what was soon going to be his, Stanley would have had a vested interest in preventing any looting on the battlefield.

Later, however, when the combatants had left the scene and most of the dead had been prepared for burial, perhaps then the scavengers arrived. There would have been rich pickings on the battlefield, as the recent discovery of Richard's silver boar badge shows. Other treasures may well have been found. We simply do not know.

In the wake of his victory Henry must have felt an amazing degree of relief. Nobody had expected him to win; he had not really expected victory himself, not once he had seen the bristling ranks of Richard's soldiers standing on the hill top. But victory it was and now, rather than a period of relaxation, the hard work began.

In the run up to Bosworth Henry had already planned that his reign should be recorded as beginning on the 21 rather than 22 August 1485, which was the date of the actual battle. When he eventually arrived in London it was a simple enough task to get this through Parliament and its purpose was clear. Anyone who had fought against Henry at Bosworth Field could be regarded as taking up arms against the lawful king and might, if the monarch chose, now be attainted for treason.

There seems to have been little objection to Henry assuming the mantle of king. He had won it by right of conquest and with Richard dead there was literally no one to oppose or challenge his position. S.B. Chrimes seems to sum up the situation quite admirably:-

> The verdict of the God of battles had confirmed such hereditary right as existed, and acclamation on the field itself rounded off the traditional procedure for attainment of the throne.
>
> (Chrimes, Page 50)

That was in the future, however, and even before he left the battlefield Henry was immersed in the issues that follow any battle.

One of the first problems to deal with was the prisoners. Many, like Lord Lovell and John de la Pole, Earl of Lincoln, had fled as soon as news of Richard's death began to circulate. They could be apprehended and dealt with later, but there were others who had stayed and given themselves up to Henry's mercy. Among these was the Earl of Northumberland.

Friends they may have once been but that was a long time ago. Northumberland's decision not to comply with Richard's orders to engage the rear guard had been instrumental in Henry's victory, but he still did not trust Henry Percy. The earl was immediately taken prisoner and before long found himself incarcerated in the Tower. There he remained until December 1485 when, with Henry now more secure on his throne, he was released, restored to his titles and appointed Warden of the East and Middle Marches.

After arranging for the prisoners to be dealt with – most were simply sent on their way, without weapons – and burial of the dead, Henry left Bosworth Field and rode to Leicester where he and his soldiers were received with great acclaim. At Leicester he paused for two days. During his stay he ordered Richard's body to be removed from public display and interred in a plain tomb within the church of the Greyfriars in the city. There it lay until the church was demolished as part of the Dissolution of the Monasteries in 1538 – and then, for many years, it vanished.

The body may have vanished, but various local legends about its fate were constantly bandied about, including the story that his bones had been thrown around the streets and then hurled into the river. Perhaps the most interesting piece of local folklore concerns the coffin of the dead king. It was apparently placed outside Leicester's White Horse Inn where, for many years, it was used as a watering trough for horses.

As soon as he could find a moment Henry had his scribes compile a circular letter which was then sent to officials across the country. In it he commanded that nobody should interfere in any way with men coming from the field of battle but allow them to proceed, untroubled, to their homes and houses. He also made it clear that he was now king and that anybody who was robbed or otherwise ill-treated should go to his sergeant at arms where he would receive fair justice. Richard was dead, this was a new regime.

Henry was making it clear in the letter that he was not prepared to allow any nobleman or official to seize the lands of the defeated Yorkists:-

> And moreover, that no manner of man take upon him to go to
> no gentleman's place, neither in the county, nor within cities
> nor boroughs, nor pick no quarrels for old or new matters;
> but keep the king's peace upon pain of hanging.
> (Henry VII, circular letter, 1485, quoted in Chrimes, p.51)

Interestingly, the punishment for any infringement of Henry's instructions was not beheading, as noblemen might expect, but hanging. In the eyes of the new king taking the land and titles of other gentlemen was nothing more than theft and the punishment was to be that meted out to any common thief.

He was bound now for London, but before he left Leicester Henry had two significant orders to send out. First, he sent a rider ahead of him with the command that Elizabeth of York, his future wife, was to be released from the Tower of London where she had been held. It was a reasonable act and certainly designed to win approval from Elizabeth and other Yorkist supporters. Once out of the Tower she was returned to the custody of her mother, Elizabeth Woodville, the widow of Edward IV, to wait on Henry's pleasure.

Henry was far from an easy touch, however, and his second order proved it. He sent a messenger to Yorkshire with the demand that Edward, the 15-year-old son of Edward's dead brother the Duke of Clarence and now the last Yorkist claimant to the throne, should be incarcerated in the Tower. Young Edward, Earl of Warwick, was duly apprehended and escorted to the most significant prison in the kingdom. He was destined to never again leave his place of internment.

Henry realised soon after his victory that he needed to feel safe on the throne – hence the imprisonment of the young Earl of Warwick – but he nevertheless made the wise decision not to take revenge on the surviving supporters of King Richard. If there were to be trials and executions they would take place after careful consideration. There was one exception, Richard's closest friend and advisor William Catesby.

Catesby had schemed and plotted to help Richard seize power, betraying those like Lord Hastings who may have been a problem, and had made himself rich in the process. Now, while Henry was still in Leicester, he was brought into the market place in the city and beheaded. His death was a rare moment of anger by Henry and an equally rare spectacle for the people of Leicester.

True to his word, Henry also began to give out the rewards he had promised. Gilbert Talbot, who had played a vital but almost unheralded part in the campaign, was one of the first to be knighted. He was accompanied by people like Rhys ap Thomas and Thomas Stanley's younger brother, Humphrey. Talbot had been seriously wounded in the battle but lived to claim his reward. As for Sir Rhys, it was nothing more than he had expected. Rewards did not stop with the nobles and great men:-

> A great many of Henry's followers were rewarded with letters
> of denizenship, extending to them the rights and privileges
> of Englishmen and freeing them from the penal enactments

of Henry IV. Even more important was the fact that the lesser offices in Wales were now granted to Welshmen.

(David Williams, p.23)

The foreign mercenaries were now dismissed – without having wreaked the havoc that Crevecouer had intended and confidently expected. Despite their troublesome nature, despite their lack of training, despite the sweating sickness they had brought with them, most of the French had done well, particularly the archers.

Henry was grateful for the French involvement and knew he would not have succeeded without them. But it was now time to send these men back to their homeland. The last thing he needed was a group of victorious and heavily armed foreign mercenaries parading all over his kingdom.

Many of the men who had flocked to his banner during his march, the Welsh in particular, also left for home before Henry set out for London. He did retain a small core of local soldiers, forming them into an elite squad that became the Yeomen of the Guard. His main supporters – Oxford, Jasper, Rhys ap Thomas and so on – had already hitched their stars to his banner and would remain with him on his triumphal journey south.

Henry had received a warm welcome in Leicester, the townsfolk eager to show their support for the new king. The fact that they had shown the same degree of approval for Richard in the days before the battle did not seem to worry them unduly. It did not worry Henry either. His upbringing may have been sheltered and, as a result, he may have been inexperienced in the ways of the world but he knew enough to realise that this was human nature. He had matured and developed during the journey from France to Bosworth. So he was not worried by the apparent fickleness of the people of Leicester.

Even the keeper of the White Boar Inn where Richard had spent his last night before setting out to fight the battle that he and everyone else thought he would win, was happy to show his new allegiance – he renamed his tavern the Blue Boar and changed the colour of the animal on his sign board. That might have given Henry a slight smile.

As Henry made his way out of Leicester he had every reason to feel proud and content. He had won his throne and the myth of good (in the form of Henry) triumphing over bad (Richard) was already beginning to take shape. Henry did not deliberately foster this idea but he was not averse to using it to his own benefit.

He knew in his heart of hearts that the battle had been won, not so much by those who fought but by those who didn't – at least not until they were sure who was going to win. The valiant performance of the Earl of Oxford had been magnificent but it was the inactivity of Northumberland and the Stanleys that had really brought him victory.

Now it was time for London and to begin making sure that the crown so hard-won would remain his for as long as he wished.

X X X

Henry's long march from obscurity to the throne did not end at Bosworth Field. Victory over Richard III was only the start of a reign that lasted twenty-four years and laid the foundations for the most powerful dynasty Britain had ever seen.

There was much to do, but first he would allow himself the luxury of the triumphal march from Leicester to the south. His route took him down Watling Street, the old Roman road, through places like Coventry and Northampton. Everywhere Henry went he received a rapturous welcome. According to Polydore Vergil people lined the roadside in town and countryside alike to cheer him on his way and to offer whatever refreshment the king and his troops required. (Vergil, Book 26)

On 15 September Henry entered the city of London and was led in a procession through the streets to St Paul's Cathedral. After giving thanks, reciting prayers and laying three standards – including the red dragon of Wales – at the door, he retired to the Bishops Palace. He then moved on to Guildford and then to his mother's house at Woking.

On Sunday 30 October 1485 in Westminster Abbey, Henry was formally crowned king. At the splendidly ostentatious coronation ceremony Jasper Tudor carried the crown, Thomas Stanley the sword of state, and the Earl of Oxford bore the train. It was a necessary expenditure, Henry felt, as the public had to see their new king in all his glory. What happened from there was a different matter altogether.

The first Parliament of the new king's reign met on 7 November, just over a week after the coronation. Its business was short and pertinent.

The first and most significant task was to remove the stigma of the attainment that Richard had placed upon Henry and his relatives. Then it had to declare him to be the lawful King of England. It was easily done.

After that Richard and twenty-eight of his supporters were attainted as traitors, even though many of them were now dead.

It was time now for more rewards. Jasper, the faithful uncle who had helped Henry through so many difficult times, was created Duke of Bedford and the Earldom of Pembroke was restored to him. The Earl of Oxford was also restored to the titles and estates he had lost under Richard and was appointed Admiral of England, Ireland and Aquitaine. He was also appointed to the post of Keeper of the Tower of London – which included taking charge of the wild animals in the Tower zoo! Thomas Stanley was created Earl of Derby; his brother William became Chamberlain of the Household and, after a short while, chief justice of North Wales.

There were other happy recipients of awards. Philibert de Chandee, commander of the French forces, was made Earl of Bath while John Savage received several minor rewards. As promised, Sir Rhys ap Thomas was confirmed as chamberlain of South Wales and steward of the lordships of Builth Wells and Brecon. Almost all of those who had defected to Henry before the battle received rewards of some type, either offices or monetary gifts.

Perhaps the greatest beneficiary, however, was the king's mother. Margaret Beaufort soon became one of the most significant figures in the king's life and, by default, in the kingdom as well. Whereas Henry had leaned heavily on Jasper during his period of exile and on the Earl of Oxford during the campaign and Battle of Bosworth Field, now he began to depend more and more on his dynamic and energetic mother.

All of the lands and titles taken from her by Richard were returned and she became the Queen Mother figure in the palace. Her rooms were always close to Henry's, either at court or when on their travels, where she could be contacted instantly and from where she could exert her influence over her son.

Despite all the odds, the House of Lancaster had triumphed. The Battle of Bosworth Field was effectively the last battle of the Wars of the Roses and nobody was more pleased than Margaret Beaufort. She had schemed, plotted and planned for this for many years. She had faced disaster and seen her hopes dashed many times. Now, at last, she had succeeded. Her son was King of England.

Chapter Eleven

The Aftermath

Henry's first few years as king were not easy. During the very first year of his reign the country was hit by an epidemic of the sweating sickness, called 'a terribyle plague' by Polydore Vergil (Vergil, Book 26). Thousands died, Vergil estimating that only 1 per cent of those afflicted managed to survive. There were some who attributed the affliction to God's displeasure; Henry simply buried his head to the disease and in due course it went away. It was to reappear many times over the next century and its cause, its severity, even its symptoms, still puzzle historians.

It was highly likely that Henry and Elizabeth of York had never met before he became king, but he was adamant that he intended to comply with his vow and marry the Yorkist Princess. This duly happened on 18 January 1486, after a period of courtship and simply getting to know each other. It was a marriage of convenience and political necessity, uniting the Houses of York and Lancaster, but surprisingly Henry and his bride fell deeply in love.

The marriage, successful as it was, was not long lasting. Even so they managed to have eight children, not all of whom survived into adulthood. Elizabeth died in 1503, leaving Henry distraught. He locked himself away for several days, seeing no one and making no decisions of state. The previous year Elizabeth and Henry's eldest son Arthur had died – possibly from a version of the sweating sickness – again leaving the king (and the queen) bitterly hurt.

During the first few years of his reign, Henry's main task was to secure his throne. Inevitably that meant military campaigns against rebels and pretenders. The first of these, led by Viscount Lovell and the two Stafford brothers, came in 1486 and was easily dealt with.

The ease with which Lovell's plot was destroyed managed to convince the remaining Yorkist supporters that, if any rebellion was going to be successful, it needed a Yorkist prince to use as a figurehead. Such a person no longer existed – or was, at least, not readily available – and the result was the creation of pretenders, not as a unified or general policy but by individual Yorkist supporters,. The idea was simple – to foster and train young men who would pretend to be genuine claimants to Henry's throne.

The first of the 'puppet masters' to find and develop a pretender was John, Earl of Lincoln, who found a suitable candidate in Lambert Simnel, the 10-year-old son of an Oxford carpenter. Simnel, it was decided, should claim to be the young Earl of Warwick, son of the Duke of Clarence and therefore nephew to the dead Richard III.

Lincoln had Simnel carefully trained by a Catholic Priest named Richard Simons. The deception was surprisingly effective and in May 1487 Lincoln even managed to achieve the amazing feat of having him crowned as King of England – not in England but in Ireland.

Henry, of course, had the real Earl of Warwick locked up in the Tower and it was a simple matter to parade the earl through the streets of London and then stand him before the Council. That effectively ended any popular support for the pretender, at least as far as the state was concerned. But the Earl of Lincoln had already displayed his colours. There was no going back for him and he now knew he had only one last chance, a military campaign and invasion.

With military and financial aid from the Earl of Kildare, the rebels duly left Ireland and landed in England to make their bid at deposing Henry. For the king it would have brought back many memories of his own landing in Milford Haven and the march to Bosworth Field. Henry knew how effective such an invasion could be and so he acted swiftly. He mobilised his troops and in June 1487 the rebels were brought to battle at Stoke.

It was a hard-fought affair during which Lincoln was killed and his German and Irish mercenaries heavily defeated. After the battle, displaying his desire to be a just and wise ruler, Henry pardoned Kildare, imprisoned the priest Richard Simons and, rather than execute him, had Lambert Simnel sent to work as a scullery boy in the royal kitchens.

Three years later a similar problem arose. Perkin Warbeck was a rather more serious pretender to the throne than the somewhat simple Lambert Simnel. He claimed to be Richard, the youngest of the 'Princes in the

Tower', and this time Henry could not publicly wheel out and display the real prince. Richard of York, like his brother King Edward V was, by then, long dead.

The moving force behind Warbeck's impersonation is not clear but it is possible that Charles III of France, perhaps as a warning for Henry to steer clear of Franco-Breton politics, was involved somewhere in the plot. Margaret of York, one of the few remaining Yorkist figures of substance, certainly had a hand in training Warbeck, whose knowledge of Richard and his brother was excellent – and clever enough to convince many people that he really was the younger of the two dead princes.

Warbeck's origins are still unclear. He was probably Flemish and had come to England to work for an English merchant. How he was recruited to become a pretender is equally as unclear, but over a nine-year period his activities cost Henry somewhere in the region of £13,000 – essentially £1 million in today's currency – to combat and eventually defeat.

After first appearing in 1490, Warbeck spent nearly eight years causing mayhem in England, Ireland and Scotland. He had a sort of charm and for some inexplicable reason managed to pull notable people, friends and supporters of Henry, into his machinations. The saddest of these was Sir William Stanley, the man who had saved the day at Bosworth Field; he became embroiled in Warbeck's schemes, was convicted of treason and went to the block in February 1495.

In 1496 Warbeck even managed to convince James IV, the Scottish King, to back an invasion of England. Support from the northern shires was, however, totally lacking and after penetrating just a few miles into English territory and taking a few lookout stations and outposts, Warbeck and his Scots retreated back across the border.

An armed uprising in Cornwall was meant to support Warbeck in the north but a couple of thousand countrymen were no match for Henry. He allowed them to march on London, then met the rebels at Blackheath, killed 1,000 of them and ended the rebellion.

After a disastrous botched attempt to land a force in Kent, Warbeck showed his true colours by leaving his soldiers and supporters to their fate while he fled to Ireland. With support beginning to ooze away he eventually over-stretched himself, landed in Cornwall with 2,000 troops and marched on London. Henry defeated him and Warbeck threw himself on the king's mercy.

Henry was indeed merciful and allowed Warbeck to live. It was not just allowing him to live; the young pretender was allowed to move around freely, although Henry's agents did keep a distant eye on the young man. In general, and for a while at least, it was not needed. Warbeck became a welcome member of the king's court, not unlike the way Henry himself had been accepted and treated in Brittany, and seemed happy enough to be feted and entertained by the great ladies and gentlemen.

It was too good to last. When he tried to flee both the court and the country, Henry realised that enough was enough. He had tried to be gracious and had had his generosity thrown back in his face. Warbeck was arrested and put in the stocks, not once but twice, where he repeated an earlier confession of his fraudulent claims. He was then sent to the Tower.

In the Tower Warbeck made the acquaintance of the Earl of Warwick and together they hatched an escape plan and a potential rebellion. It seemed that Warbeck simply would not learn. The two miscreants were apprehended and in November 1497 Perkin Warbeck was executed – by hanging rather than the axe. The earl followed him, to the executioners block in his case, a few weeks later.

X X X

The years were not kind on Henry. He aged badly, the handsome young man who had beguiled the French and Breton courts slipped quietly and quickly away. In his place came the miserly, haunted figure that posterity loves. Why there should be such a relatively quick change in his physical appearance is not clear. Perhaps it was the pressure of constantly looking over his shoulder to see where the next challenge for his throne was coming from, or possibly the loss of long-standing friends and allies. Whatever it was he grew haggard and gaunt as the business of kingship seemed to weigh him down.

Several deaths affected him badly. William Stanley's betrayal was like a knife under the ribs, while the murder of Henry Percy, the Earl of Northumberland, in 1489 was proof that no one was really safe in any part of the kingdom. His Uncle Jasper, the man who had always been by his side, died at Thornbury Castle in December 1495. Not until he was gone did Henry realise how much he had depended on the old man.

Henry himself died at eleven o'clock on the evening of 21 April 1509. He was 52 years old and had ruled for nearly twenty-four years. Only at the end, when it was almost too late, did he feel secure on his throne. His health had suffered and the final five or six of his eventful years had been particularly painful as he went steadily downhill:-

> The symptom were all too familiar; tuberculosis, combined with the suffocating quinsy. He fought on but, as he had done before, he sensed death approaching.
>
> (Penn: Winter King, p.333)

They had been dramatic and troublesome times as the king strove to secure his dynasty and help England recover, economically and socially, from the carnage of the Wars of the Roses. There must have been moments when he sat back and wondered why he had bothered. If so, they would have been quick, fleeting thoughts. He was born to be king. It was his destiny.

The root of the security he so cherished lay, Henry knew, in finance. Until England was financially secure the country would always flounder. Taxation and raising money therefore became a central focus of his reign, his tax collectors – Epsom and Dudley in particular – becoming hated figures as they went about their work. To some extent this was from where the common perception grew and developed that Henry was not popular with his subjects. Such a belief has more than a sprinkling of truth about it.

He was not loved in the way that his son, Henry VIII, was loved – at least in the early stages of his reign – but Henry Tudor knew he was not there to be loved. He was there to do a job and if that meant upsetting his subjects, so be it. He and the dynasty certainly became rich. By the time of his death it has been estimated that Henry was personally worth £1.5 million, a figure that is close to £1 billion in today's currency.

Henry also took a great interest in developing England as a trading nation. He was particularly active in assisting the wool trade grow to an extent where it could stand effectively against the rigorous trade policies of the Netherlands and its flourishing wool business. Such achievements were unspectacular, but they were essential elements of the country's growth.

At the end of the day, however, Henry's greatest achievement was in the way he provided stability for his country and for his people. He knew that was what he had to do, even if his subjects sometimes failed to appreciate his efforts. Many of those efforts would only reach fulfilment in the years after his death when, in the sixteenth century, the greatness of the country and its people in things like exploration and navigation, poetry and drama, finally reached a zenith:-

> Such a development would have been inconceivable without the intermediation of Henry of Richmond's regime. Not for him the vast egoisms of his son Henry nor the gloriations of his grand-daughter Elizabeth. But without his unspectacular statecraft their creative achievements would have had no roots.
>
> (Chrimes, p.321)

Opinions vary as to whether Henry VII was the last of the medieval monarchs or the first of the modern ones. Was he a leftover from the Middle Ages or a true Renaissance prince? The question is one of those imponderables, a little like scholars discussing the number of angels that could dance on the point of a needle. Arguably he did not have enough money to become a true Renaissance prince, but he was unhappy with any remnants of feudal powers left in the country. He was an active supporter of the arts and even brought in the great Renaissance scholar Erasmus to coach and teach his son Henry.

Henry was Henry, as simple as that. Without his influence, without his intuitive understanding of what the country needed, there could well have been a return to the chaos of the Wars of the Roses.

Let's finish with a couple of those hypothetical, maybe even rhetorical questions that historians hate. No apologies, they're something that have to be asked. Without Henry VII would there have been playwrights like William Shakespeare and Ben Jonson? Would there have been explorers like Walter Raleigh and Francis Drake or poets such as John Donne? Would Dowland, Campion and Byrd have even begun composing? It remains an interesting if impossible dilemma, and one which would require a book on its own to come close to an answer.

Conclusion

Henry VII, the first monarch in a dynasty that was to rule over England for 122 years, is perhaps the least known of all the Tudor kings and queens. That is something of a shame because he remains a fascinating and beguiling character.

If you take the time and the trouble to look at his life he will emerge as a man of courage and ambition, a man of self-doubt and modesty. He could be merciful or he could be ruthless, depending on the situation and whatever he felt was required. But he could equally be seen as someone who was also filled with humanity.

His journey to pull on and bear the crown of the country he undoubtedly loved began with his birth in Pembroke Castle in 1457. It took twenty-eight years before he fulfilled his aim to re-establish the House of Lancaster on the throne of England, twenty eight years filled with failure, frustrated hopes, peaks and troughs and, eventually, an almost unbelievable success on the battlefield. Following in his footsteps gives you a good indication of the character and personality of the man and those he encountered. The story reads like a novel.

That novel or story, that passage of history if you must view his life in the traditional way, culminates in Henry's march to Bosworth and a battle that he should never have won. Everything that a good story needs – in particular, the three elements of storytelling, people, place and problems – can be found here in the life of Henry Tudor and his incredible gamble that took him from the shores of Milford Haven to a blood-drenched field close to Market Bosworth.

There are those who view Henry in a somewhat different light. He, they say, not Richard murdered the Princes in the Tower and this, the first Tudor monarch, went on to conduct a relentless crusade to destroy all rival claimants to his throne. By the reintroduction of the Court of Star Chamber he established:-

> an instrument of Tyranny – used to punish people who had not broken any law but had merely done actions that the judges deemed to be morally reprehensible.
>
> (Gwynne, p.172)

That is perhaps an overly simplistic view of Star Chamber which did, in many instances, produce genuinely good judgements. Overall there seems to be little evidence to back up such claims, but as with everything, you can always find an answer to any question as long as you look at it in the way you want. However, Henry was the ultimate pragmatist and would have done whatever was necessary to ensure stability for the country and a safe heritage for his children – which maybe, just maybe, leaves the door ajar.

The Battle of Bosworth Field has been seen as the classic case of good versus evil. That is probably an over-simplification but there can be no doubt that Richard III has become, for most of us, the epitome of evil – which naturally leaves Henry on the other side of the debate. It is another element of the story and, remember, all good stories need a villain. Thanks to 'The Ballad of Bosworth Field', the works of Polydore Vergil and of Shakespeare, Richard has certainly been cast in this role.

The final act in the story, the tragedy if you like, of Henry and Richard concerns the last Plantagenet King of England rather than the first Tudor one. Richard's body went missing after 1538 when the Abbey of the Greyfriars was pulled down as part of Henry VIII's dissolution of the monasteries. For nearly 500 years nobody knew the whereabouts of his remains.

Then, in September 2012, the medieval skeleton of a man clearly killed in battle was discovered within the site of the former Greyfriars Friary Church in Leicester. As the entire world now knows, the old building was in the process of being converted into a car park.

Wounds to the skull, the back of which had been hacked off, and other injuries seemed to indicate that these were the remains of Richard III. Interestingly – and thereby ending many years of debate – the skeleton had a severe curvature of the spine. If this was indeed Richard, then perhaps Shakespeare's play and the mesmerising Olivier interpretation of the character were not so far off the mark after all.

Conclusion

After anthropological and genetic testing proved that the skeleton really was that of Richard, on 26 March 2015 his remains were reinterred in Leicester Cathedral. It was a fitting conclusion to the mystery of Richard's disappearing remains.

Whatever Richard III did in his brief reign – the seizure of the crown, the possible murder of the two princes, executions without trial – was surely done to prevent a return to the Wars of the Roses. If that is so, then he was no worse and no better than Henry.

The actions of both men can be interpreted in any way you like, but one thing remains crystal clear – whatever they did, whatever they thought, has to be considered in the context of the times. Any other way of looking at them is to demean their actions and to destroy one of the greatest stories in British history.

Bibliography

Primary Sources (fifteenth and sixteenth centuries)

Anon 'The Ballad of Bosworth Field', fifteenth-century poem
Anon 'The Crowland Chronicles', possibly 1486
Raphael Holinshed 'Chronicles of England, Scotland and Ireland', Vol 6, 1577
John Leland 'De Ulris illustribus: On Famous Men', sixteenth century, new
    edition edited by James Carley, Toronto, 2010
Polydore Vergil 'Anglica Historia', Books 23–25 and Book 26, written
    1512–13, published 1534

Reports

12th Report of the Historical MSS Commission, Appendix, Part IV, Page 7

Secondary Sources
Books

Anon *A Short History and Guide to Pembroke Castle* Five Arches Press,
    Tenby, 1977
Carradice, Phil, *Pembroke: For King and Parliament* Pembroke Town
    Council, 1993
Charles, B.G., *The Place Names of Pembrokeshire* Vol 1 and 2, National Library
    of Wales, Aberystwyth, 1992
Chrimes, S.B., *Henry VII* Yale University Press, New Haven, 1999
Griffiths, Ralph A., (ed) *Sir Rhys ap Thomas and His Family* originally published
    1620s (Anon), this edition University of Wales Press, Cardiff, 2018

Gwynne, N.M., *Gwynne's Kings and Queens* Ebury Press, London, 2018

Laws, Edward, *The History of Little England Beyond Wales* originally 1888, republished 1995 by Cromwell Press/Haverfordwest Library, Haverfordwest, 1995

Miles, Dillwyn, *Portrait of Pembrokeshire* Hale, London, 1984
   Castles of Pembrokeshire Pembrokeshire Coast National Park, Haverfordwest, 1979

Owen, H., and George Owen, *The Description of Pembrokeshire* Vol 1, 1892, Vol 2 1897, originally written by George Owen and published mid-sixteenth century

Penn, Thomas, *Winter King* Penguin, London, 2011

Skidmore, Chris, *Bosworth: The Birth of the Tudors* Phoenix, London, 2013

Williams, David, *A History of Modern Wales* John Murray, London, 1950

Articles

Welsh History review, Vol 2 (1964–65), pp.173–180, article by S.B. Chrimes

History Review, June 2018, article by Julian Humphreys, pp.47–50

Web Sites

www.dailymail.co.uk/news/article

https://en.wikipedia.org/wiki/Battle_of_Bosworth-Field

Interviews/Letters

Letter from Roger MacCallum, April 2018 (held by author)

Interview with Peter Lewis, April (transcript held by author)

Acknowledgements

Many people helped in the creation of this book, far too many to list and record. To them my heartfelt thanks. However the following are deserving of special mention. I owe them a debt of gratitude that can never be fully repaid:-

Roger MacCallum, who assisted not only with the technical details, but also in his other role as an author and geologist was unfailingly generous with his ideas and theories about the exact location where Henry Tudor came ashore. Brilliant, Rog, as always.

Peter Lewis, former Sheriff of Haverfordwest, who spent a morning with me detailing his 1985 walk from Dale to Bosworth.

Pat Lewis, Peter's wife, who filled me in on her role as 'ground staff' and harbinger during Peter's walk back in 1985.

My two sons, Andrew and Douglas – one a traditional Lancastrian, the other an out and out Yorkist – for invaluable discussions and comments during the writing of the book.

My elder son Andrew for his drawing of Henry as a young man – based on a sixteenth-century sketch.

About the Author

Phil Carradice is a poet, novelist and historian with over sixty books to his credit. His most recent works are *The Cuban Missile Crisis: Thirteen Days on an Atomic Knife Edge* and *The Bay of Pigs*, both for Pen and Sword's Cold War series, and *Bloody Mary*, the story of Mary Tudor's infamous reign. He is a regular broadcaster on radio and regularly takes creative writing classes for children and adults.

Index